Dick and Fitzgerald

Book of Riddles and Five Hundred Home Amusements

Dick and Fitzgerald

Book of Riddles and Five Hundred Home Amusements

ISBN/EAN: 9783337255008

Printed in Europe, USA, Canada, Australia, Japan

Cover: Foto ©Andreas Hilbeck / pixelio.de

More available books at **www.hansebooks.com**

DICK & FITZGERALD,

In the Clerk's Office of the District Court of the United States, for the Southern
District of New York.

FIVE HUNDRED RIDDLES

HOME AMUSEMENTS.

———✦✦✦———

PART I.

RIDDLES, CHARADES, ENIGMAS, REBUSES, TRANS-POSITIONS, AND CONUNDRUMS.

AMONG the innocent recreations of the fireside, there are few more commendable and practicable than those afforded by what are severally termed Anagrams, Charades, Conundrums, Enigmas, Puzzles, Rebuses, Riddles, Transpositions, etc.

As it is next to an impossibility to glean from dictionaries the precise distinctions between, and properties of, Enigmas, Charades, &c., I have taken upon myself the task of describing the difference which does exist, for the enlightenment of all who take an interest in such matters. You are doubtless aware that Messrs. Webster, Johnson, and Walker have very considerately informed us that —" an enigma is a kind of riddle,"—" a riddle is an enigma,"—" a charade is a riddle, usually in verse,"—and that " a rebus is a sort of riddle." Now, what are we to infer from these descriptions,—that they are all one and the same thing? No, certainly not. Therefore, with all due deference to those who may think or state to the contrary, I will depict that which I consider to be the precise nature of each of these words : for that they have every one a separate signification I verily believe ; and, with this impression, I will do my best to clear away the mist which at present hangs over them.

Charades, Rebuses, Conundrums, &c., are with many persons favorite recreations. In the construction of several of them, considerable ingenuity is displayed; they are not, in all cases, the production of mere witlings and holiday rhymesters; for more than one author of celebrity, doubtless, in some of those sportive moments when the mind relaxes from graver pursuits, to toy and dally with comparative trifles, has contributed his mite towards the great fund of riddles now in circulation. One of the most clever and best written among the following collection has been ascribed to the pen of the late Lord Bryon :—we allude to the lines on the letter H. A work of this size does not contain a tithe of all the Enigmas, Charades, &c., now current; we have therefore endeavored to make a judicious selection of a few from the mass.

RIDDLES.

It may be asked, What is a riddle?—Ah! what is it? that's just the rub! Well, then, it is a queer affair, without shape, size, humanity, compassion, breath, or sex. It is caressed, abused, courted, slighted, jostled, hostled,—and, notwithstanding all that is said against it, universally looked upon as a welcome guest when it is not in a dull mood. The oldest riddle on record is that put forth by Samson (Judges xiv. 14)—"Out of the eater came forth meat, and out of the strong came forth sweetness." His solution is well known, as it is explained in the same chapter.

No doubt there are many riddles which should have been handed down to posterity, that deserved this distinction,—but that ascribed to Cleobulus, one of the seven wise men of Greece, deserves to be recorded: it is said to have been composed about the year 705 B. C. "There is a father, with twice six sons : these sons have thirty daughters a-piece, parti-colored, having one cheek white and the other black, who never see each other's face, nor live above twenty-four hours." His solution was "The year."

How we have puzzled over some of the good old riddles of yore, and when their solutions have been whispered, half in mirth and half in fear at our wrath, we have laughed at our very stupidity, and wondered how any person could fail to discover them.

What a batch now crowd upon us—'tis fearful to contemplate! But we shall dash them off as they pass in review, commencing with—

1.
M. Voltaire's Riddle.

What is the longest and yet the shortest thing in the world; the swiftest, and the most slow; the most divisible, and the most extended; the least valued, and the most regretted; without which nothing can be done; which devours every thing, however small, and yet gives life and spirit to all things, however great?

2.

My number, definite and known,
Is ten times ten, told ten times o'er;
Though half of me is one alone,
And half exceeds all count and score.

3.

I am the centre of gravity, hold a capital situation in Vienna, and as I am foremost in every victory, am allowed by all to be invaluable. Always out of tune, yet ever in voice; invisible, though clearly seen in the midst of a river. I have three associates in vice, and could name three who are in love with me. Still it is in vain you seek me, for I have long been in heaven, and even own lie embalmed in the grave.

4.

Four people sat down in one evening to play:
They played all that eve and parted next day.
Could you think, when you're told, as thus they all sat,
No other played with them, nor was there one bet:
Yet, when they rose up, each gained a guinea,
Tho' none of them lost to the amount of a penny.

5.

Here is a riddle which is old, but good, and may be new to some of our readers. We will introduce it, making a few alterations, such as we deem improvements:—

The Wonderful Prophet.

To be seen at Westchester, near New York, a strange and wonderful prophet, whose generation was before the creation of Adam. He was not the Wandering Jew, nor the son of Noah, nor the old Levite, nor John the Baptist; for he was certainly before them all. The Scriptures make mention of him, particularly in St. Mark, St. Luke, and St. John; so that we may believe that he is no impostor. He knows not his parents; he never lay upon his mother's breast; his beard is such as no man ever wore. He goes barefooted, like a grave friar. He wears no hat in winter or summer, but often appears with a crown upon his head. His coat is neither knit nor spun, silk nor hair, linen nor woollen. He is a teetotaller. He prefers an humble dwelling to a palace. He is very watchful. He sleeps not in bed, but sits in a singular kind of chair, with his clothes on. He was with Noah in the Ark, and was alive at the Crucifixion. Nearly all the world hear him. He once preached a short sermon, which convinced a man of his sins, and caused him to weep most bitterly. Though he never rides on horseback, he is in some respects equipped as horsemen are. He is an advocate for early rising, though he never retires to bed. His prophecies are so true, that the moment you hear his voice, you may know what is approaching. Now who is this prophet, and what doth he foretell?

6.

Sir T. Wyatt, the author of the following two riddles, holds a place among our English poets. He was the friend of the accomplished Earl of Surrey, and was considered a brilliant ornament of the court of Henry the Eighth, by whom he was employed as envoy to more than one European court. His son was executed for rebellion in the reign of Mary.

> A lady gave me a gift she had not,
> And I received her gift which I took not.
> She gave it willingly and yet she would not;
> And I received it, albeit I could not.

If she give it me I force not,
And if she take it again I grieve not.
Consider what this is and tell not,
For I am fast sworn, I may not.

7.

Vulcan my father, Minerva me taught,
Nature my mother; craft nourished me year by year,
Three bodies are my food; my strength it is naught.
Anger, wrath, waste, and noise are my children dear.
Guess, friend, what am I, and how I am wrought;
Monster of sea or land, or of elsewhere?
Know me, and use me, and I may thee defend,
But if I be thine enemy I may thy life end.

8.

Perfect with a head, perfect without a head, perfect with a tail, perfect without a tail, perfect with either, neither, or both.

9.

My head and tail both equal are,
My middle slender as a bee,
Whether I stand on head or heel
'Tis all the same to you or me;
But if my head should be cut off,
The matter's true, although 'tis strange,
My head and body severed thus,
Immediately to nothing change.

10.

Beneath the skies a creature once did dwell,—
So sacred writers unto us do tell,
He lived, he breathed, in this vain world, 'tis true,
Though he ne'er sinn'd, or any evil knew;

He never shall in Heaven's high kingdom dwell
Or e'er be doomed to feel the pangs of Hell;
Yet in him an immortal soul there was
That must be damned—or, live among the just.

11.

What is that which every one can divide, but no one can see where it has been divided?

12.

What is that which we receive without thanks? which we enjoy without knowing how? which we bestow on others without knowing where it is to be found? and which we lose without being sensible of its loss?

13.

Hold up your hand, and you will see what you never did see, never can see, and never will see.   What is this?

14.

There is a word of three syllables, from which, if you take away five letters, a male will remain; if you take away four, a female will be conspicuous; if you take away three, a great man will appear; and the whole word presents you with a great woman. What is this word?

15.

Name two English words, one of which, being of one syllable only, shall contain more letters than the other of five syllables.

16.

Which English word contains the greatest number of letters?

17.

What English word is that, the letters of which, three in number, may be placed in any order, and at each transposition form a well-known word?

18.

What word of six letters admits of five successive elisions, leaving at each abbreviation a well-known word?

19.

What word of six letters contains six words besides itself, without transposing a letter?

20.

Which were made first, elbows or knees?

21.

What is majesty deprived of its externals?

22.

If a woman were to change her sex, what religion would she be of?

23.

What thing is that which is lengthened by being cut at both ends?

24.

I consist of four letters. Multiply my *first* by five, and you will find my *last ;* halve my *first*, and place the half as my *third ;* my *second* is a figure of itself worthless; my *whole* has no place in the name of the book in which this appears.

25.

There are two words only in our language wherein the five vowels follow in successive order. Which are they?

26.

There are two youths mentioned in Scripture, who, in degrees of consanguinity, were so remarkably circumstanced, that their father was their grandfather—their mothers were their sisters— their sisters were aunts—and they were each other's uncles! Who were they?

27.

What word is that composed of five *letters*, from which, if you take two, one remains ?

28.

Is there a word in the English language that contains all the vowels ?

29.

What is that which we often return yet never borrow ?

30.

What is that which cats have, but nothing else has ?

31.

What is that which makes every thing visible but is itself· unseen ?

32.

How many soft-boiled eggs could the giant Goliah eat upon an empty stomach ?

33.

What is that which is often brought to table, often cut but never eaten ?

CHARADES.

THE CHARADE is a poetical or other composition, founded upon a word, each syllable of which constitutes a *noun*, and the whole of which word constitutes another noun of a somewhat different meaning from those supplied by its separate syllables. Words which fully answer these conditions are the best for the purposes of charades; though many other words are employed. In writing, the first syllable is termed "*My first*," the second syllable, "*My second*," and the complete word, "*My whole*." The following is an example of a poetical charade:

The breath of the morning is sweet;
The earth is bespangled with flowers;
And buds in a countless array
Have oped at the touch of the showers.

The birds, whose glad voices are ever
A music delightful to hear,
Seem to welcome the joy of the morning
As the hour of the bridal draws near.

What is that which now steals on *my first*,
Like a sound from the dream-land of love,
And seems wandering the valleys among—
That they may the nuptials approve?

'Tis a sound which *my second* explains,
And it comes from a sacred abode,
And it merrily trills as the villagers throng
To greet the fair bride on her road.

How meek is her dress, how befitting a bride,
So beautiful, spotless, and pure;
When she weareth *my second*, oh, long may it be
Ere her heart shall a sorrow endure.

See the glittering gem that shines forth from her hair,
'Tis *my whole* which a good father gave,
'Twas worn by her mother with honor before—
But *she* sleeps in peace in her grave.

'Twas her earnest request as she bade them adieu,
That when her dear daughter the altar drew near,
She should wear the same gem that her mother had worn
When she, as a bride, full of promise stood there.

The answer is *Ear-ring*. The bells *ring*, the sound steals upon the *ear*, and the bride wears an *ear-ring*. Charades may be sentimental or humorous, in poetry or prose; they may also be *acted*, in which manner they afford considerable amusement.

1.

In various states I exist; and when Morn
   Is painting the clouds, I lend him my aid;
In autumn the spider's frail web I adorn;
   I am found in the streamlet when daylight doth fade.

'Mid the Alps, in their wonderful glaciers I'm found;
   In the ice of the Poles—in the shade of a well—
In the many-hued Iris—I surely abound;
   In the beautiful tears of compassion I dwell.

Of the nectar, far-famed of the gods, I was part;
   I dwell in the joy-giving words of the earth;
I dwell in each flower, and I dwell in man's heart;
   And I dwell in the mists which at morn have their birth.

Thus various my *first.* Now my *second's* a game,
   Indulged in by many—too many, I fear—
Whose fortunes are ruined; they, covered with shame,
   Suffer agony wild as their homes they draw near.

To think of the dear ones—their happiness gone—
   The wife broken-hearted, hence homeless and poor;
All ruined by folly too frequently shown,
   To deeds such as this doth this *second* allure!

When my *first* and my *second* are joined, you'll perceive
   The name of a battle-field, glorious, but dread,
For thousands were caused by its carnage to grieve
   For their kinsmen, whose blood in that battle was shed.

2.

The Lovely Alice.

The lovely Alice has dressed her hair;
Her form is sylph-like—her face is fair:
To meet her the gay young knight advances;
Asks for her hand through various dances;—
Asks for her hand for "ever and a day,"
And trembles lest my *first* her lips should say.

The gay young knight calls forth his steed,
Of Arab race, of purest breed;
Hopes his fair Alice will accept the horse,
Made for his dear to canter o'er the course,

Free from all blemish—a splendid creature reckoned,
And vows in him she'll never find my *second*.

The lovely Alice looks with eager eye
Upon the steed—his paces longs to try.
My *second* mention not, she says, " I've tried
Successfully to curb a courser's pride:
In such I ne'er can be esteemed my *whole*—
Leave that to nuns—I'll tame his fiery soul."

3.

A plunge is heard—he will drown, he will sink;
He calls for my first, oh! haste to the brink.
A ship at that moment appears in view;
My *second* is there amongst the crew.
The man is saved, and at once doth exclaim,
Ah! my *whole* will rejoice to embrace me again;
For she's a companion whom I ever find,
In joy or in sorrow, most loving and kind.

4.

Two gamblers were " sitting"
    Striving to cheat each other,
And, by a cunning trick, my *last*
    Had raised a fearful bother.
The one who lost he looked my *first*,
    But he who won assumed my *whole*,
Which little did the luckless one
    Amid his bitter grief console.
Since both were rogues, we will not screen them—
There was not my *second* to choose between them.

5.

My *first* often contains my *second* ; my *second* often dreads my *first* ; and though there is not a possibility of its following, runs away from it. By the account of many, my *whole* will never be so happy as in its present condition.

6.

My *first*, nor book nor volume named
    Contains more leaves than most;

My *next*, when certain crops are claimed,
  Still stalks a numerous host:
My *whole*—a creeping flower so fair,—
Regales the eye and scents the air.

7.

My *first* is to ramble; my next to retreat:
My *whole* oft enrages in summer's fierce heat.

8.

My *first* do all nurses possess,
  And dandle my *second* upon it;
My *whole* is a part of the dress
  Attached to the cap or the bonnet.

9.

My *first* oft preys upon my *second* :
My *whole* a bitter shrub is reckoned.

10.

My *first* in fruit is seldom rare;
My *second* all relations are:
My *whole* is only earthenware.

11.

My *first* dreads my *second*, for my *second* destroys my *first*,
while many delight in my *whole*.

12.

In every hedge my *second* is,
  As well as every tree;
And when poor school-boys act amiss,
  It often is their fee.

My *first*, likewise, is always *wicked*,
  Yet ne'er committed sin:
My *total* for my first is fitted,
  Composed of brass or tin.

13.

My *first's* a prop, my *second's* a prop, and my *whole's* a prop.

14.

What I do, what I do not, and what you are.

15.

My *first* is equality; my *second*, inferiority; my *whole*, superiority.

16.

He can seldom obtain my *first*, who labors for my *second* ; and few like to do my *whole.*

17.

My *first* is of no use without my *second* ; and my *whole* is to be seen every day in Broadway.

18.

My *first* is wise and foolish; my *second*, the physician's study; my *whole*, the pleasantest ornament of a house.

19.

My *first* communicates to the human race joy and sorrow, love and hate, hope and despair; my *second* retains what is gross, and rejects what is delicate; my *whole* is reflective.

20.

My *whole* is under my *second*, and surrounds my *first.*

21.

When you stole my *first*, I lost my *second* ; and I wish you may ever·possess my *whole.*

22.

Addressed by the Right Hon. Charles Fox to the Duke of Northumberland.

I'll employ my *first* in praise of my *second*, if you'll give me my *whole*.

23.

A Letter—By Mr. Fox.

Permit me, madam, with the profoundest respect, for once to come uncalled into your presence, and, by dividing myself, add greatly to my consequence.

So exalted am I in the character of my first, that I have trampled upon the pride of kings; and the greatest potentates upon earth have bowed down to embrace me; yet the dirtiest kennel, in the dirtiest street, is not too foul to have me for its inmate.

In my second, what infinite variety! I am rich as the eastern Nabob, yet poor as the weeping object of your benevolence—I am mild and gentle as the spring, yet savage as the wintry blast—I am young, beautiful, and blooming, yet deformed and wretched. From the highest authority, madam, I dare prove I am your superior, though few are the instances that prove it, and ten thousand the proofs against it. I am ——; but you are tired, and wish my re-union; it is done, and my consequence is lost, and I have no other merit than remaining, as at first, your most obedient servant,   THE WHOLE.

24.

My *first*, the source of wit and mirth supreme,
  With thee, my friends, 'tis pleasant to enjoy;
Oh! may my *next* with wholesome plenty teem,
  Free from those things that tempt but to destroy

And may my *whole* no sordid hoard contain,
  No hidden bag—no dainty mouldering lie—
By avarice taught inactive to remain,
  And feed alone the greedy miser's eye!

25.

Three mighty powers affect mankind,
Three mighty things I trow they be ;
The *first* a gift—a free-will grant ;
The next a wish, or else a want ;
A loss, the *last* of all the *three.*

The *first*, a gift without consent,
Yet prized above all things below ;
'Tis like a wave—'tis like a flower—
'Tis like a dream—or like an hour ;
It brings us joy, and brings us woe.

The *first* and *second* still produce
The one the other, mutually ;
The *second*—like the honey sweet—
Like glowing beams of summer's heat ;
Yet bringeth cares and misery.

Or with, or yet without the first,
My *whole* could no existence find ;
'Tis like a ghost—'tis like a sleep ;
It ends our pains, and makes us weep ;
It ends the woes of all mankind.

26.

His heart was sad, and his foot was sore,
When a stranger knocked at the cottager's door ;
With travel faint, as the night fell down,
He had missed his way to the nearest town,
And he prayed for water to quench his thirst,
And he showed his purse as he asked for my *first.*
The cotter was moved by the stranger's tale,
He spread the board, and he poured the ale :
" The river," he said, " flows darkly down
Betwixt your path and the lighted town,
And far from hence its stream is crossed
By the bridge on the road that you have lost ;
Gold may not buy, till your weary feet
Have traversed the river and reached the street,
The thing you ask ; but the wandering moon
Will be out in the sky with her lantern soon ;
Then cross o'er the meadow, and look to the right,
And you'll find my *second* by her light."

My *second* shone like a silver floor,
When the traveller passed from the cotter's door;
He saw the town on its distant ridge,
Yet he sighed no more for the far-off bridge;
And his wish of the night soon gained its goal,
For he found my *first* when he reached my *whole.*

ENIGMAS.

ENIGMAS are compositions of a different character, based upon *ideas* rather than upon words, and frequently constructed so as to mislead, and to surprise when the solution is made known. Enigmas may be founded upon simple catches, like Conundrums, in which form they are usually called RIDDLES, such as—

"Though you set me on foot,
  I shall be on my head."

The answer is, *A nail in a shoe.*

The following enigma and its history, which is given in " Sirr's Ceylon," deserves to be more generally known, as it was composed by one of the native Ceylonese kings, Kumara Dhas, a prince of great learning, who reigned A. D. 517; and it illustrates the peculiar style of the time. Both riddle and answer are looked upon as master-pieces, as the number and position of the letters in the original, in both enigma and reply, strictly agree, the latter being written by Kalidhas, the celebrated poet and friend of the monarch. Naturally in translation the peculiar beauty is lost, but we give it as a curious and interesting poetical specimen.

The riddle of Kumara Dhas :—

"By beauty's grasp, in turmoil uncomposed,
  He is kept a prisoner, but with eyes unclosed."

The elucidation by the poet Kalidhas :—

"Although closed at night the lotus keeps the bee,
  The dawn will see him gay, unhurt, and free."

The circumstance which occasioned these lines is thus recorded in the native annals :—The King was in the habit of visiting a female, celebrated alike for her wit, beauty, and captivating manners ; and one evening, whilst in her company, remarked a bee alight on a pink lotus, which closed upon and imprisoned the insect. The monarch immediately wrote the two lines on the wall, intending to compare his own situation with that of the captive bee, as he was enthralled by the woman's wiles ; stating that whoever would complete the stanza should have any request granted which they might choose to prefer. Shortly after the monarch quitted the female's abode, Kalidhas, who was also in the habit of visiting the house, entered, and seeing the writing on the wall, immediately concluded the verse in the same style. The wretched woman, to obtain the promised reward, murdered the poet and buried him under the floor. But when the monarch saw the reply, he immediately recognized the style and writing of his favorite, Kalidhas. The murder was discovered, the corpse disinterred, and, by order of the king, a most magnificent pile was prepared, whereon the body was to be burned with all the rites and ceremonies which belonged solely to royalty. When the funeral pyre was ignited, the grief and mental agony of Kumara Dhas, at the loss of his friend, overcame all other feelings, and he rushed into the flames, and was consumed with the body of the poet Kalidhas. History also recorded that the five queens of Kumara Dhas voluntarily immolated themselves on the same spot shortly afterwards ; and we believe this to be the only record of royal widows in Ceylon sacrificing themselves at the tomb of their spouses.

1.

Ancient Enigma.

The ancients fabled a monster whom they named the SPHINX, and whom they described as having the head and breasts of a woman, the body of a dog, the tail of a serpent, the wings of a bird, the paws of a lion, and a human voice. This monster, it was said, was sent into the neighborhood of Thebes by Juno, who wished to punish the family of Cadmus. It was further stated,

that he laid this part of Bœotia under continual alarms, *by proposing
Enigmas,* and devouring the inhabitants if unable to explain them.
Also, that as the calamity of this monster was become an object
of public concern, and as the successful explanation of an enigma
would end in the death of the Sphinx, Creon promised his crown
and Jocasta to him who succeeded in the attempt.   The enigma
proposed was this :—

" What animal in the morning walks on four feet, at noon on
two, and in the evening on three?"

Œdipus solved the enigma—on which the monster dashed his
head against a rock, and perished.

2.

My aunt, at her mansion on Mulberry Green,
Was a kind-hearted lady as ever was seen ;
For true hospitality, friendship, and mirth,
There was not a more good-natured creature on earth.
She wrote to me thus:—" My dear Nephew, come down.
You need relaxation from duties in town ;
Dogs, horses, and guns, at your service shall be,
If you like to enjoy a snug fortnight with me.
But as I (upon second thoughts) think you'll prefer
A young friend, to a 'crusty old woman like me,'
You may bring one or two good companions—and all
Shall find a warm welcome at Mulberry Hall."
   Well, I thought, such a kind invitation as this
(With such pleasures in prospect) t'were folly to miss;
So with cheerful Bob Goodwill and Theodore Bright,
I spent the first week in incessant delight.
And said, " Aunt, I have profited finely, you see,
By the friendly indulgence you granted to me ;
I have strictly adhered to your liberal tone,
And have made your nice house and your servants my own."
Three words, of one syllable each, she replied,
And I canter'd off briskly—my blushes to hide.
   I soon joined my friends, and the hounds in full cry,
And no one could feel more delighted than I.
The breeze was refreshing—the sun's early ray
Was expanding around into beautiful day;

The scent of the woodbine, the lark in loud song,
So charmed me, as (heedless) I galloped along,
That, careless of all but the hounds and the horns,
We fell in a ditch full of briers and thorns.

With scrambling, and kicking, and pulling, my horse
Was soon out of this awkward dilemma—of course
But, alas! in the struggle I nearly was stript,
And every seam in my coat was unript.

My mortification at seeing my aunt,
(In my woful condition) describe it I can't;
She laughed, as my prison I made my way through,
And held out my coat, and said, " What shall I do?"

Her reply was the very same words as before
Pronounced—the real words are for you to explore.

3.

Enigma by Lord Bryon.

'Twas whispered in heaven, it was muttered in hell,
And echo caught faintly the sound as it fell:
On the confines of. earth 'twas permitted to rest,
And the depths of the ocean its presence confessed.
'Twill be found in the sphere when 'tis riven asunder,
Be seen in the lightning and heard in the thunder.
'Twas allotted to man with his earliest breath,
Attends at his birth, and awaits him in death ; .
It presides o'er his happiness, honor, and health,
Is the prop of his house, and the end of. his wealth.
Without it the soldier and seaman may roam,
But woe to the wretch who expels it from home.
In the whispers of conscience its voice will be found;
Nor e'en in the whirlwind of passion be drowned.
'Twill not soften the heart, and tho' deaf to the ear,
'Twill make it acutely and instantly hear.
But in shade let it rest, like a delicate flower—
Oh, breathe on it softly—it dies in an hour.

4.

Enigma by Cowper.

I am just two and two, I am warm, I am cold,
And the parent of numbers that cannot be told;
I'm lawfully unlawful, a duty, a fault,

Exceeding dear, good for nothing when bought;
An extraordinary boon, and a matter of course,
And yielded with pleasure when taken by force.

5.

Five simple letters do compose my frame;
And, what is singular, when viewed, my name
Forwards and backwards will be found the same;
  When I'm discovered, you will plainly see
  What the proud peer and peasant soon will be.

6.

A shining wit pronounced, of late,
That every acting magistrate
Is water in a freezing state.

7.

Formed long ago, yet made to-day,
  Employed while others sleep;
What few would ever give away,
  Or any wish to keep.

8.

Formed half beneath and half above the earth,
We, sisters, owe to art a second birth;
The smith's and carpenter's adopted daughters,
Made on the earth to travel o'er the waters.
Swifter we move, as tighter we are bound,
Yet neither touch the water, air, nor ground.
We serve the poor for use, the rich for whim,
Sink when it rains, and when it freezes, swim.

9.

I'm rough, I'm smooth, I'm wet, I'm dry;
My station low, my title high;
The king my lawful master is;
I'm used by all, though only his.

10.

There is a thing was three weeks old,
  When Adam was no more;

This thing it was but four weeks old,
When Adam was fourscore.

11.

We are two brothers, born together, who seldom touch the earth, though we often go to the ground; although we never eat fodder, buy, sell, or barter, we may be said to be interested in the *corn* laws.

12.

Never still for a month, but seen mostly at night.

13.

In spring, I am gay in my attire; in summer, I wear more clothing than in spring; in winter, I am naked.

14.
Unsolved Enigma.

I'm short and I'm tall, I'm broad and I'm narrow;
Like a ram's-horn I'm curled, and yet straight as an arrow;
I'm not in the water, and yet I declare
That I can't live on earth, and I die in the air;
And for fire—I be burnt if I ever go there!
You would faint but to see me, so hideous my face is;
Yet my features are fair as a juvenile's graces!
My voice is a roar, yet so sweet is its flowing,
It sets every bosom with ecstasy glowing.
My youth would enchant e'en the stoutest beholder,
And yet I'm as old as the world is—and older!
To describe myself farther there's little requiring,
To your patience and mine, 'twould be equally tiring:
Yet, ere I cease rhyming, this hint let me give ye,
And then to your guessing, at once I shall leave ye:
Imagine all opposites, all that most strange is,
A thing still the same, through a million of changes;
Which at once can in New York and Tartary be:
And if such you discover—be sure it is me.

15.

The following Enigma has been attributed to a late Archbishop

of Canterbury. It is said to have a meaning, which no one independent of the author has been able to solve :—

> I sit high on a rock when I'm raising the wind,
> But the storm once abated, I'm gentle and kind;
> I have kings at my feet who wait but my nod,
> To lie low in the dust where my footsteps have trod;
> I never have been but one night in the dark,
> And that was with Noah afloat in the ark;
> I've been often on earth, but am known but to few,
> The Gentile detests me—I'm pork to the Jew;
> My weight is three pounds; my length is a mile.
> But when you have found me, you'll say with a smile—
> That my first and my last are the best in the Isle.

16.

By George Canning.

> There is a word of plural number,
> Foe to peace and tranquil slumber.
> Now, any word you choose to take,
> By adding *s* you plural make;
> But if an *s* you add to this,
> Strange is the metamorphosis,
> Plural is plural then no more,
> And sweet what bitter was before.

17.

> In fair Creation's dawn I was on earth,
> Skimmed o'er the flood—roved o'er the mountain brow;
>   In Eden's groves I played at Adam's birth,
> And near that spot, so hidden, hover now.
>
>   My colors merry as the rainbow's dyes,
> My form as various as the shadows gray
>   In early hours that see the sun arise,
> Or Eve's cool moments at the close of day.
>
>   I dwell with diamonds in Golconda's mine;
> My life is wrapt in shades of darkest hue;
>   I peep through leaves and tendrils of the vine,
> And all may see me in th' ethereal blue. ·
>
>   I stand on pinnacles of towering height,
> Enter Earth's deep recess at man's control;

In battle-fields I mark the cannon's flight,
And hold my place till darkness shrouds the whole.

My influence over man is far and wide :
On sea,—in every land, he owns my power;
  And yet I aid him in each hour of need,
And pleasure yield him in his gloomiest hour.

I dwelt in Eden, as I said before,
And yet as then I was, I am to-day;
  Perhaps,—but yet I must not tell thee more—
Reader, *you* value me—what am I, say?

18.

I am always in trouble, yet always in joy;
I am always in poverty, yet ne'er out of employ;
Though you view me in terror, I'm naught you need fear,
'Tis but once in a month that I ever appear.

I have been in confinement a great length of time—
In all prisons and dungeons, and yet not in crime;
You have seen me alone, I will venture to tell,
And you've seen me in thousands and millions as well;
Yet when to your view is this riddle unfurled,
You'll be free to confess there's but one in the world.

19.

A Vision.

It was on a cold frosty evening, when the wind whistled
round the corners of the house, and roared down the chimney,
that I sat in my old arm-chair reading. I laid down my book,
and with an inexpressible sense of comfort, gazed in the fire.
Gradually my mind wandered; the faces my imagination had
pictured in the fire became more and more indistinct, till at last
I fell into a kind of waking dream. Methought I saw before
me a wilderness, where the wild beast roamed free in the endless
solitudes, and grass and weeds grew unrestrained; where the
birds built their nests in the oak and beech trees which towered
above the rest, and feared not the encroaching hand of man.
But an old veteran, whose hair was gray, and whose body was

2

bent by the weight of years, came by. He looked on the waste, and waved his staff on high. When I looked again, I saw the huge monarchs of the forest falling beneath the stroke of the axe; and where once stood a giant oak, now stood an emigrant's hut, and several little children were playing before the door. Again the staff waved—the hut had disappeared—the trees encumbered the ground no more; for in their place stood cottages, corn-fields, and ploughed lands. The husbandmen were busy at work, some sowing, and some following the plough. The little children I had seen before were now grown to manhood, and tilled lands of their own. Once more the old man flourished his staff—what a change did I see! Corn-fields, cottages, husbandmen, and all had vanished, and their place was occupied by a large manufacturing town. The streets resounded with the din of carts and carriages; bells tolled from steeples of magnificent churches; and where once existed a swamp was now a noble edifice. Day and night the manufactories echoed with the busy hum of labor and the song of the artisan. But was there no alloy to this pleasurable scene? Alas! that I should record it! There was; and in the place of soberness, cleanliness, and innocence, there were drunkenness, poverty, and filth, and theft, and murder! Alas! that these crimes should pollute the track of civilization—but so it is. I awoke, and with the first sensations of my dream, there had gone out my fire, and the lamp was flickering and nearly extinguished; so I hurried shivering to bed. Reader, who was the old man I saw in my dream? While seeing him, I was losing him; and when I had again found him, I had lost him.

20.

Not room, but loss of room by me is got;
Yet you will have no room where I am not;
To give you comfort is my end and plan,
In cold to shelter you, in heat to fan.
I am at once a thoroughfare and screen,
And in all families act as go-between.

On other strength I still depend and hinge,
But, though I shut and open, never cringe;
My common size is seven feet high by three,
Yet all mankind pass and repass by me.

21.

Four things there are, all of a height,
One of them crooked, the rest upright.
Take three away, and you will find
Exactly ten remains behind.
But if you cut the four in twain,
You'll find one-half doth eight retain.

22.

I am seen in the desert and found in the hall,
And Adam beheld me long after his fall;
I sleep in the pyramids vast, and the hill
Where the ark found a refuge containeth me still.

I was long seen at Nineveh—Egypt's my own!
The prophets have made me their moral and crown.
I care not for potentate, heed not the wise,
My name is as old as the earth or the skies.

The meanest of slaves and the proudest of kings
May become as myself on the moth's silken wings;
I am what I make, and create what I am;
Behold me an inmate of Isis and Cam!

For with lore of the sages I love to reside,
And oft clothe with a garment the offspring of pride;
I am known in all climates—I sweep with the gale,
Over desert and mountain, and always prevail.

With the dead I lie down and contentedly sleep,
While maidens above me assemble to weep;
I'm the spring of all life and the winter of fame—
Ye sibyls domestic, come tell me my name.

23.

In every gift of fortune I abound,
In me is every vice and virtue found;
With black, and blue, and green, myself I paint,
With me an atheist stands before a saint;

Far before nature I make art precede,
And before sovereigns give the poor the lead;
Many who bear the name of learned and wise,
Did I not help them, you would oft despise.

Nay more; without my grasp, together bound,
The king, the beggar, and the noble's found.
In one thing I excel the proudest lord—
You always may depend upon my word.

24.

I never was, but always am to be;
None ever saw me—you may never see;
And yet I am the confidence of all
Who live and breathe on this terrestrial ball.

The princely heir, his honors not yet blown,   _
Still looks to me for his expected throne;
The miser hopes I shall increase his wealth;
The sick man prays me to restore his health.

The lover trusts me for his destined bride;
And all who hopes or wishes have beside.
Now name me, but confide not, for believe
That you and every one I still deceive.

25.

I have a face, eyes, nose, mouth, and ears; yet I see not—smell nothing—taste nothing, and hear nothing. When my eyes are directed to you I see nothing. Made by a sunbeam, I am destroyed by a sweep of the hand. In darkness was I born, and I never saw the light. I am to be found on the most fashionable promenades, and in almost every parlor. I am but a shadow, yet I am capable of reflection. If it were not for light I'd never be, yet one-half of you don't know it.

26.

Two men, with their two wives and two sons, stand thus related to each other: the men are each other's fathers and sons, their wives' fathers and husbands, and their children's fathers and grandfathers; the women are the children's mothers and sisters, and the boys are uncles to each other. How can this be, and yet the parties be lawfully married?

27.

Five hundred begins it, five hundred ends it,
Five in the middle is seen;
The first of all letters, the first of all figures,
Take up their stations between.
My *whole* was a king of very great fame;
If you wish to know who, you here have his name.

28.

Figures, they say, won't lie; but here
Is something either false or queer.
I find that, in my family,
One taken from two still leaves me three,
And two from two, by the same score,
Leaves a remainder of just four.

29.

What is that which, supposing its greatest breadth to be four inches, length nine inches, and depth three inches, contains a solid foot?

30.

'Tis said of lawyers Grab and Clinch,
They take an ell when you offer an inch;
But I can do a smarter thing—
Give me an ell, I will make it ring.
If for advice you come to me
When you are ill, I call for the fee.
If any road you chance to wend,
You think you've reached the very end,
I come and give it such a turn,
You find there's something yet to learn;
If to the inn you seek for rest,
I chuck you in a box or chest.

The beggar's rags I make so proud,
He of his garments boasts aloud.
The aged and infirm with me
Lose caution and timidity ;
For, young or old, to every one
I furnish, if not muscle, bone.

REBUSES.

REBUSES are a class of enigmas generally formed by the first,
sometimes the first and last, letters of words, or of transpositions
of letters, or additions to words. Dr. Johnson, however, represents
Rebus to be a word represented by a picture. And putting the
Doctor's definition and our own explanation together, the reader
may glean a good conception of the nature of the Rebus. Example :—

The father of the Grecian Jove ;
A little boy who's blind ;
The foremost land in all the world ;
The mother of mankind ;
A poet whose love-sonnets are
Still very much admired :—
The *initial* letters will declare
A blessing to the tired.

Answer—*S*aturn ; *L*ove ; *E*ngland ; *E*ve ; *P*etrarch. The initials form *sleep*.

1.

Take him whose daughter, with a pitying eye,
Saw the poor babe in cold and danger lie ;
And in that eye beamed love and mercy mild,
For she with true compassion saved the child.

And next that priest who showed such fervent zeal,
That he the truths of Scripture did reveal ;
Arranging in their course these books sublime,
And fixed the holy canon for his time.

And now that pious man before us bring,
Whose office, cup-bearer to Persia's king,
Had given him wealth and rank, but still his pity
Was shown in solemn prayer for his poor city.

And next that scoffer who aloud would call,
While the poor Jews were building up their wall—
"That which ye build may soon be overthrown
E'en by a fox, though it be made of stone."

Now that good man of Judah, one of three
Who would not to the image bow the knee,
On which the king, with fierce and deadly ire,
Had cast him bound into the burning fire.

And next in order now I must require
Our father Abraham's most honored sire.

Now that good man who had for forty years
Judged Israel, but who mourned with bitter tears
The errors of his sons, their wicked jeers.

And next that king who ably did preside,
And governed well and happily, till pride
Leading him on—a leper was—and died.

That man of Judah who, by God's command,
Was sent by Moses to the promised land.

And lastly, he who did in pieces break—
Lest others should an idol of it make—
The brazen serpent, which by God's command
Had been set up by Moses in the land.

The initials of these names will bring to mind
What in the Bible we shall always find;
But though it does to us much truth impart,
And is *the law*, 'tis only found in part
Of God's own book; and this you may depend—
'Tis nearer the beginning than the end.

2.

I've either read, or heard it said,
   That Jupiter one day
Was sorely vexed, and much perplexed—
   "For what?" I hear you say.

The case was this :—he'd neither miss
    Nor master to him born,
And so, 'twas said, he smote his head,
    Like one that's quite forlorn;
When straight arose, before his nose,
    A goddess, fair and tall:
Whom doubtless you can bring to view -
    And name her too withal.

Another name, and one of fame
    (A classic man must own),
In days of yore this goddess bore,
    In ancient Athens known.
And by again another name
    This goddess went as well;
Which you can find, if you're inclined :
    'Tis spelt with double L.
Now if I'm right, you have in sight
    Initials that will make
A picture geographical,
    And really no mistake.

3.

A hundred and fifty, if rightly applied,
To a place where the living did once all reside;
Or a consonant joined to a sweet singing bird,
Will give you a name that you've oftentimes heard,
Which, 'mong your friends, at least one person owns:
It's the rival of Smith, and as common as Jones.

4.

To three-fourths of a cross, add a circle complete;
Then, let two semi-circles a perpendicular meet;
Next, add a triangle that stands on two feet;
Then, two semi-circles, and a circle complete.

ANAGRAMS.

OF the various devices for family and social amusement, none are more ingenious than anagrams. The term itself is derived from two Greek words, *ana*, again, back, and *gramma*, a letter; and the meaning is, the turning of a word or sentence so as to form others. Transposition is another name applied to the same pastime, and is equally expressive. On a small scale this is frequently done. If you have a box of letters, you may take from it an L and a V, and an E and an I, and desire to have made more words than there are letters. This sounds strange, but it is easily accomplished by transposition of the letters. Live, vile, evil, veil, Levi, all consist of the precise letters before us. Or you may take two O's, an E, a W, a D, an R, and an N, and desire to have one word made. If placed rightly, ONE WORD will be formed. But anagrams are far more interesting if the changes of the words bear some relation to each other, and yet more when they can be made to apply to historical events or characters.

The making of anagrams has been the pastime of not a few of the profoundest minds. To take one word, and by transposing all the letters to bring out one or more complete words, is an exercise requiring no little ingenuity. Perhaps one of the best is that which finds the phrase, *Honor est a Nilo*, or " Honor is from the Nile," in the name of its hero, Horatio Nelson.

The following are some of the most remarkable :

Transposed	*forms—*
Astronomers	No more stars.
Catalogues	Got as a clue.
Elegant	Neat leg.
Impatient	Tim in a pet.
Immediately	I met my Delia.
Masquerade	Queen as mad.

Astronomers—Moon-starers.
Democratical—Comical trade.
Gallantries—All great sin.
Lawyers—Sly wares.

2*

Misanthrope—Spare him not.
Monarch—March on.
Old England—Golden land.
Punishment—Nine thumps.
Presbyterian—Best in prayer.
Penitentiary—Nay I repent it.
Radical reform—Rare mad frolic.
Revolution—To love ruin.
Telegraphs—Great helps.

TRANSPOSITIONS.

TRANSPOSITIONS are a species of anagram, and are sometimes a source of much fun in the EVENING CIRCLE. The following are excellent examples:

1.

A gentleman who was paying his addresses to a lady, at length summoned up sufficient courage to ask if they were agreeable to her, and whether he might flatter himself with a chance of ultimate success. The lady replied—"*Stripes!*" telling the gentleman to transpose the letters so as to form out of them another word, which word was her answer. The reader who can find out the word, needs never fear being *nonplussed* by a lady; those who cannot must either persist till they overcome the difficulty, or may give up all thoughts of wooing.

2.

I AM COMPOSED OF SIX LETTERS:
Without my 1, 2, 3, I am part of a lock.
Without my 4, I am the miser's god.
Without my 5, 6, I am a member of the Roman Catholic church.
Without my 1, 4, 5, 6, I am a preposition.
Without my 2, 3, 4, 5, I am a pronoun.
Without my 3, 4, 5, 6, I am the initials of one of the United States.
My whole is an animal of South America.

3.

Read me aright, I'm useful to cooks;
But by transposition, draw boys from their books;
Again transposed, then me you would shout
Most lustily after a thief, I've no doubt. ;
Transpose but once more, and I may be found
In each street of the city, both steadfast and sound.

CONUNDRUMS.

CONUNDRUMS.—These are simple catches, in which the sense is playfully cheated, and are generally founded upon words capable of double meaning. The following are examples :

1.

Which are the two smallest insects mentioned in the Scripture?

2.

How is it that Methuselah was the oldest man, when he died before his father?

3.

What is the difference between Joan of Arc and Noah's ark?

4.

Why are sinners like corn and potatoes?

5.

Why are Cashmere shawls like deaf persons?

6.

When a boy falls into the water, what is the first thing he does?

7.

Why is a New York milkman like the fish that swallowed Jonah?

8.

What did Adam and Eve do when they were expelled from Eden?

9.

Why is a conundrum like a monkey?

10.

Why is a horse half way through a gateway like a cent?

11.

What is the difference between a young girl and an old hat?

12.

What grows the less tired the more it works?

13.

How does a pitcher of water differ from a man throwing his wife over a bridge?

14.

Why is a watch-dog larger at night than he is in the morning?

15.

What is the difference between a cashier and a schoolmaster?

16.

Why are stout gentlemen prone to melancholy?

17.

Why is a melancholy young lady the pleasantest of all companions?

18.

Why was Herodias' daughter the *fastest* girl mentioned in the New Testament?

19.

What did the seven wise men of Greece do when they met the sage of Hindoostan?

20.

Why is the letter K like a pig's tail?

21.

Why do old maids wear mittens?

22.

Why is green grass like a mouse?

23.

What is the difference between a grandmother and her infant grandchild?

24.

Why does a miller wear a white hat?

25.

Why is a nail, fast in the wall, like an old man?

26.

Why are washerwomen the most inconsistent of persons?

27.

What is the difference between killed soldiers and repaired garments?

28.

Why is a shoemaker like a true lover ?

29.

What is the difference between Solomon and Rothschild ?

30.

What is the difference between a successful lover and his rival ?

31.

What was Eve made for ?

SOLUTIONS TO THE RIDDLER.

RIDDLES.

1. Time.
2. Thou-sand.
3. The letter V.
4.   Four merry fiddlers played all night,
               To many a dancing ninny;
             And the next morning went away,
               And each received a guinea.
5. Chanticleer, or the Cock.
6. A Kiss.
7. A Gun.
8. A Wig.
9. The figure 8.
10. The fish that swallowed Jonah.
11. Water.
12. Life.
13. That the little finger is not so long as the middle finger.
14. He, Her, Hero, Heroine.
15. Strength—Ideality.
16. Disproportionableness.
17. Ear—Are—Era—Rae—Aer (Latin for air)—Rea (a river).
18. Brandy—brand—bran—ran—an—a.
19. Herein—he—her—here—ere—rein—in.
20. Knees—beasts were created before men.
21. A jest, m-ajest-y.
22. She would be a he'then.
23. A Ditch.
24. Gold.
25.   In ABSTEMIOUS the five vowels you'll find
            In successive order, as your question enjoined;
            But, as for the other, I've not recollected—
            Oh, stay, 'tis FACETIOUS, which can't be objected.

26.   Moab and Ben-ammi, by Scripture, 'tis clear,
      Were the sons and the grandsons of Lot,
      Whose mothers, their sisters and aunts also were,
      Each was uncle to each,—was he not?

27. Stone.
28. Yes, unquestionably.
29. Thanks.
30. Kittens.
31. Light.
32. One, after which his stomach is not empty.
33. A pack of cards.

CHARADES.

1. Water-loo.	14. Love-ly.
2. No-vice.	15. Peer-less.
3. Help-mate.	16. Re-store.
4. Grim-ace.	17. Chair-man.
5. School-boy.	18. Book-case.
6. Wood-bine.	19. Pen-sive.
7. Gad-fly.	20. Waist-coat.
8. Lap-pet.	21. Hearts-ease.
9. Worm-wood.	22. Pen-sion.
10. Pip-kin.	23. Foot-man.
11. Fox-chase.	24. Cup-board.
12. Candle-stick.	25. Life-time.
13. Foot-stool.	26. Bed-ford.

ENIGMAS.

1. MAN: in the *morning*, or days of infancy, he crawls, or walks on "all *fours*;" at *noon*, or in the days of youth and middle age, he uses *two* feet only; in the *evening*, or in his old age, he requires the support of a staff, so that he may be said to walk upon *three* feet.

2. So it seems.—Sew its seams.
3. The letter H.
4. A kiss.
5. Level.
6. Justice—(*just-ice*).
7. A bed.
8. A pair of skates.

9. Highway.
10. The moon.
11. The feet.
12. The moon.
13. A tree.

14. Probable Solution of Enigma 14.

1. Water may be short and tall, broad and narrow.

2. The crests of waves are "*curled :*" water is straight as an arrow when at rest.

3. Water is not *in* the water, as it is the very substance itself.

4. Water cannot live *on* the earth, or *in* the air, as it sinks into the first, and cannot remain in the latter, but soon falls in the form of rain.

5. This line seems to be a mere threat of never "*going to the fire.*"

6. The sea is very "*hideous*" in a storm,

7. Yet very beautiful in a calm.

8, 9. The waves "*roar*" in a storm, but "*sweetly flow*" in a calm.

10, 11. In the first chapter of Genesis, we are told that "the Spirit of God moved on the *face of the waters*" *before* the creation of the world.

17. Water is still the same, through a "*million of changes,*" and may at "*once be in New York and Tartary.*"

15. Probable Solution of Enigma 15.

Firm on the rock of Christ, tho' lowly sprung,
The Church invokes the Spirit's fiery tongue,
Whose gracious breathings* rouse but to control
The storm and struggle in the sinner's soul.
Haply, erelong his carnal conflicts cease,
And the storm sinks in faith and gentle peace.
Kings own its potent sway, and humbly bow,
The golden diadem upon their brow.
Its saving voice with mercy speeds to all,
But oh! how few to quicken at its call!
Gentiles the favored little flock detest,
And Abraham's children spit upon their vest.
Once only, since Creation's work, has night
Curtained with darkening clouds its saving light,
What time the Ark majestically rode,
Unscathed, upon the desolating flood.
The silver weighed† for it in all its strength,
For scarce three pounds when counted, whilst its length,

---

* The rushing mighty wind. Acts ii. 2.

† The weight of thirty pieces of silver was, according to Zechariah (chap xi. 12), about three pounds.

Traced in the Prophet's view with measuring reed,
Squared just a mile,* as Rabbis are agreed.
And now I feel entitled well to smile,
Since Christ Church† bears the palm in all our isle.

16. Cares-s (Caress).

17. Light. The second line of the third verse contains a reference to *coal*, in which, certainly, is the life or first principle of light.

The second line of the fourth verse refers to the Davy and other lamps carried into coal-mines.

18. The letter O.

19. Time.

20. A door.

21. XIII., VIII.

22. Dust.

23. A Dictionary.

24. To-morrow.

25. A Daguerreotype.

26. The two men had been widowers, and married each other's daughters.

27. DAVID.

28. Two children from two parents make 4.

29. A shoe.

30. The letter B
Of ell, it makes bell.
" ill,   "   bill.
" end,   "   bend.
" in,   "   bin.
" rags,   "   brags.
" old,   "   bold.
" one,   "   bone.

REBUSES.

1.—1. Pharaoh.—*Genesis* ii. 9.
2. Ezra.—*Ezra* vii. 12; see also the note at the end of the Book of Ezra, by Dean Prideaux.
3. Nehemiah.—*Nehemiah* i. 11, and i. 5—11.
4. Tobiah.—*Nehemiah* iv. 3.
5. Abednego.—*Daniel* iii.

* Ezekiel, chap. xlii. 20. The square of the temple in the New Jerusalem was 2,000 cubits, equal to one mile.
† Christ Church, Oxford, England.

6. Terah.—*Genesis* xi. 27.
7. Eli.—1 *Samuel* iv.
8. Uzziah.—2 *Chronicles* xxvi.
9. Caleb.—*Numbers* xiii. 6 and 17.
10. Hezekiah.—2 *Kings* xviii. 4, and *Numbers* xxi. 8, 9.
PENTATEUCH,
the first five Books of Moses. The Pentateuch is also called "The Law."
2. Minerva; Athene; Pallas.—MAP.
3. C-L-ark, or C-lark (Clark).
4. TOBACCO.

TRANSPOSITIONS.

1. The word *Stripes* transposed so as to form *Persist.*
2. Monkey.
3. Pots—tops—stop—post.

CONUNDRUMS.

1. The widow's *mite* and the wicked *flee.*
2. His father was translated.
3. The one was Maid of Orleans, the other was made of chittim wood.
4. Because they have eyes, yet see not, and ears, yet hear not.
5. Because we cannot make them here (hear).
6. He gets wet.
7. Because he finds a profit (prophet) in the water.
8. They *raised Cain.*
9. Because it is far-fetched and full of nonsense.
10. Because it is head on one side and tail on the other.
11. Merely a difference of time—one has feeling and the other has felt.
12. A carriage-wheel.
13. One is water in the pitcher, and the other is pitch her into the water.
14. Because he is *let out* at night, and *taken in* in the morning.
15. One tills the mind, while the other minds the till.
16. Because they are men of size (sighs).
17. Because she is always a-musing.

18. Because she got *a-head* of John the Baptist on a *charger*.
19. Eight saw sages (ate sausages).
20. Because it is the latter end of pork.
21. To keep off the chaps.
22. Because the cattle eat it (cat'll eat it).
23. The one is careless and happy, the other is hairless and cappy.
24. To keep his head warm.
25. Because it is in firm (infirm).
26. Because they put out tubs to catch "soft" water, when it rains "hard."
27. The former are dead men, and the latter are men-ded (dead)!
28. Because he is faithful to the last.
29. One was king of the Jews, the other Jew of the kings.
30. The one kisses his miss, and the other misses his kiss.
31. Because she was Adam's Express Company.

———

Thus ends our Key to the Riddler. Our young readers, we doubt not, have very frequently referred to it, in perusing the various questions and puzzles whic h precede it, in order to save themselves the trouble of tasking their ingenuity to discover the solutions. They ought not, however, to have recourse to the Answers, until they have made frequent attempts to solve the Riddles. Some persons cannot, without considerable difficulty, find the proper answer to an Enigma or a Rebus; while others, of no greater general acuteness, do so with ease. It is no proof, therefore, of inferiority, not to be able to reply to a quaint Conundrum so quickly as another. Many young people have displayed much ingenuity in the construction of different sorts of Riddles in rhyme,—they are, in general, the most happy in solving those of others. The admirers of these frequently amusing trifles, consider opposition in their component parts, or curious combinations, to be most essential in the construction of good Riddles.

PART II.

NATURAL MAGIC; OR, RECREATIONS IN SCIENCE, EMBRACING CURIOUS AMUSEMENTS IN MAGNE-TISM, MECHANICS, ACOUSTICS, CHEMISTRY, HY-DRAULICS, AND OPTICS.

Fireside Mesmerism.

Take a gold ring—the more massive the better—but your wife's wedding-ring will do, if you are so lucky as to have one. Attach the ring to a silk thread about twelve inches long; fasten the other end of the thread round the nail-joint of your right fore-finger; and let the ring hang about half an inch above the surface

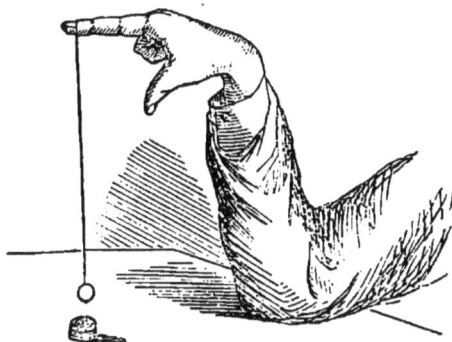

FIG. 1.

of the table, on which you rest your elbow to steady your hand. Hold your finger horizontally, with the thumb thrown back as far as possible from the rest of the hand.

If there be nothing on the table, the ring will soon become stationary. Then place some silver (say three half-dollars) immediately below it, when the ring will begin to oscillate backwards and forwards, to you and from you. Now bring your thumb in contact with your forefinger (or else suspend the ring from your thumb), and the oscillations will become transverse to their former swing. Or this may be effected by making a lady take hold of your disengaged hand. When the transverse motion is fairly established, let a gentleman take hold of the lady's disengaged hand, and the ring will change back to its former course. These effects are produced by the *Od* (or animal magnetic) currents given forth by the hands of the experimenters. Instead of silver, you can suspend the ring over your left forefinger with similar results.

Hearing with the Teeth.

That faculty which we call " hearing," can be as well conveyed to the mind by means of the teeth as the ear. Curious as this

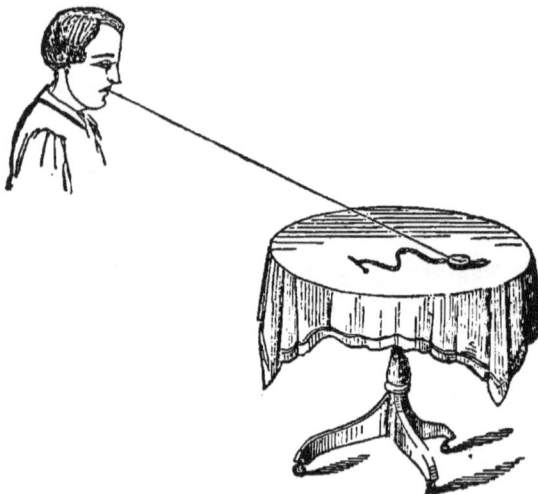

FIG. 2.

assertion may appear, it is easy to prove it by the following simple experiment. Lay a watch upon a table, glass side downwards; then stand so far from it that you cannot in the ordinary way hear the ticking. Now place one end of a small deal stick (say six feet long) upon the back of the watch, and grip the teeth to the other; with the fingers close each ear, to exclude all external noise; the beat of the watch will then be as audible as if placed against the ear. All other sounds can be conveyed in the same manner, no matter how long the stick is; for instance, if one end is put upon a pianoforte in a sitting-room facing a garden, and the stick is thirty or forty feet long, extending to the farther end of the lawn or walk; if the instrument is ever so lightly played, " the tune" will be instantly distinguished by any person applying the teeth to the opposite end of the stick.

To Raise Fire by Command.

A vessel containing a certain white powder is placed upon the table by the wizard—the man who is held in great awe by the juveniles on account of his seeming supernatural powers, and yet beloved by them because he affords them much pleasure by the exhibition of his talent, to say nothing of the bon-bons, apples, oranges, almonds, and sugar-plums, which he causes to issue from an apparently empty drawer, or handkerchief, and upon which they are allowed to feast. This said wizard having placed the above-mentioned powder on the table, now advances, waving his wand and uttering the magic words, " *Cassafello presto, aldiboron-tiphoskophorniosticos,*" when lo! of a sudden the room is lit up with a brilliant light, so effulgent that it dims the eyes of the spectators! The secret is this:—The powder is composed of equal weights of loaf-sugar and chlorate of potash, separately reduced to fine powder, and then well mixed together. This is placed in some vessel, such as a cup, or in fact anything that will prevent the fire from injuring the table. When this powder is touched with the least drop of sulphuric acid, it will instantly burst into a flame; if, therefore, the end of the glass rod be dipped in the acid immediately before use, it will, on being brought into contact with the deflagrating powder, cause it to ignite.

To Light a Candle without Touching the Wick.

Let a candle burn until it has a good long snuff, then blow it out with a sudden puff, a bright wreath of white smoke will curl up from the hot wick; now, if a flame be applied to this smoke, even at a distance of two or three inches from the candle, the

FIG. 3.

flame will run down the smoke and rekindle the wick in a very fantastic manner. To perform this experiment nicely, there must be no draught or " banging " doors while the mystic spell is rising.

To Place a Glass of Water in such a Position that no one can Remove it without Upsetting it.

Propose a wager with some one that you will fill a glass with water, and place it on the table in such a manner that he cannot move it to another place without spilling the whole of its contents.

Then fill a glass with water, and having laid over it a piece of paper which covers the water and the edges of the glass, place the palm of the hand on the paper, and taking up the glass with the other hand, turn it upside down very quickly, and place it on a perfectly flat part of the table. Gently withdraw the paper; the water in the glass will remain in it, since the air cannot enter; and the person with whom you have bet cannot move it in any way without allowing the air to enter, and consequently spilling the water.

NOTE.—It is on the same principle that a bottle of liquid well corked is perfectly safe, even though there may be several holes in the bottom; but the moment you uncork it, the liquid rushes out through those holes.

Hat Measurement.

Very few people are aware of the height of the crown of a stove-pipe hat. A good deal of fun may be created by testing it

FIG. 4.

in this way: Ask a person to point out on a wall, with a cane,

3

about what he supposes to be the height of an ordinary hat, and he will place the cane usually at about a foot from the ground. You then place a hat under it, and to his surprise he finds that the space indicated is more than double the height of the hat.

Fire upon Ice.

If a piece of potassium be pressed with a penknife upon a cake of ice, the chemical action of the materials is so energetic that they burst into a beautiful reddish-purple flame, and a hole is made in the ice where the potassium came in contact with it.

Another way to make a fire is the following:—Make a hole in a block of ice with a hot poker; pour out the water, and fill up the cavity with spirits of camphor; the spirit may then be set on fire. It will have the singular appearance of " ice in flames."

To Set a Combustible Body on Fire by the Contact of Cold Water.

Fill a saucer with water, and let fall into it a piece of potassium, of the size of a peppercorn (which is about two grains). The potassium will instantly become red hot, with a slight explosion, and burn vividly on the surface of the water, darting at the same time from one side of the vessel to the other, with great violence, in the orm of a red-hot fire-ball.

To make Wine or Brandy Float on Water.

To perform this seeming impossibility take a tumbler half full of water, and placing a piece of thin muslin over the top of the same, gently strain the brandy or wine through the muslin, and it will remain on top of the water.

The Magic Egg.

Take a pint of water, and dissolve in it as much common salt as it will take up; with this brine half fill a tall glass; then fill up the remaining space with plain water; pouring it in very carefully down the side of the glass, or into a spoon, to break its fall. The pure water will then float upon the brine; and, in appearance, the two liquids will seem but as one. Now, take another glass, and fill it with common water. If an egg be put into this, it will instantly sink to the bottom, see Fig. 6; but if, on the contrary, the egg is put into the glass containing the brine, it will sink through the plain water only, and float upon that portion which is saturated with salt, appearing to be suspended in a very remarkable and curious manner, see Fig. 5.

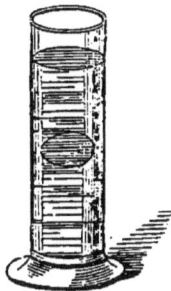 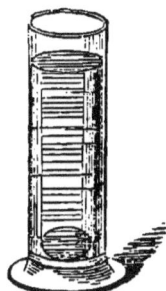

FIG. 5.   FIG. 6.

This trick has caused much astonishment when publicly exhibited, although its principle could be explained by every housewife who, before "pickling," tries the strength of the brine by observing if an egg will float on it.

Which is the Boiled Egg?

Boil an egg hard; when quite cold place it among a dozen, or any number of others, "the more the merrier." Now ask your friends to tell you which is the boiled egg. This they will be

unable to do from outward appearance ; indeed, there is but one
way to ascertain it with certainty, except that of " peeping at the
inside," which is by spinning them.   Those which are unboiled,
and semi-liquid inside, will spin with a sort of waddling motion,
while the boiled, or solid egg, will spin like a top, and even " go
to sleep."

Musical Flame.

Fit a good cork into a wine bottle ; burn a hole through the
cork with a round iron skewer, and into it fix a piece of tobacco-
pipe about eight inches long.   Put into the bottle about two or three
ounces of zinc, in slips, such as the waste cuttings from a zinc-
worker; now pour water on to the zinc until the bottle is rather
more than half full ; then add about three parts of a wineglassful
of sulphuric acid (oil of vitriol) ; this causes a rapid effervescence

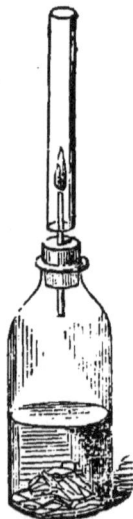

FIG. 7.

at first, but which subsides to a moderate and continuous boiling
for a lengthened period ; as soon as the boiling is regular the cork

with the pipe through it may be inserted into the bottle. If a light be placed to the end of the pipe, a flame will be produced, which will continue to burn so long as there is any visible action in the bottle. This flame is the ignited hydrogen gas (water gas) resulting from the decomposition of water by the acid and zinc, and as such is an exceedingly interesting experiment. Now, to be musical, procure a glass or metal pipe about sixteen or eighteen inches long, and from half to three quarters of an inch in diameter; place the tube over the flame, and allow the pipe to be about three to five inches up the tube, which will act as a kind of high chimney: it must be held perfectly steady and upright at a particular distance up the tube, which varies according to the size of the flame. A beautiful sound is thus produced similar to an organ pipe. This sound, or " musical flame," varies in note according to the diameter of the tube, being deeper or more bass as the tube is increased in size. By using various-sized tubes, different sounds are thus readily produced. The true explanation of this singular experiment remains yet to be solved.

To balance a Stick on the edge of a Glass of Wine.

Take a stick a foot long (a little more or less), and two pen-knives of *equal weight;* stick them by the point on a level on each

FIG. 8.

side of the stick, parallel, at the distance of about three inches from the end you place on the glass, and be careful that the curves in the handles are turned towards the glass, as represented in the accompanying engraving. You may then drink off the wine, and the stick will still continue its extended position, and not fall off. Great care should be taken to have the knives equally balanced, or the experiment will not be successful.

To Stand an Egg Upright.

The unceremonious manner in which the Great Navigator performed this feat, by breaking one end, is familiar to all who have read the anecdote of "Columbus and the Egg." Evidently at that time it was considered *impossible* to stand an egg on its point. Such, however, is not the case. By taking an egg (a long one is the best), and well shaking it, so that the yolk may be broken and mixed with the white, it can be balanced, by any one with a "steady hand," upon its broad end. A piece of glass, or slate, or any smooth and even surface, is best adapted for this experiment, called the Sentinel Egg.

The Doubled Coin.

Half fill a glass of water, and put a dime or a quarter into it ; cover the glass with a plate, upon which place one hand, while you hold the glass with the other ; turn the glass upside down, so that none of the water may escape ; place it on a table, and you will see the coin at the bottom larger than it is in reality, and another will appear, of the natural size, a little above it.

To Burn the Poker in the Candle.

With a good rasp, file off an ounce from the fire end of a poker. The iron filings produced are perfectly combustible, as may be proved by sprinkling them over the flame of a candle. As they descend into the flame they take fire, each particle burning like a star—producing, in fact, miniature fireworks. Iron filings derived from any other source burn in the same way; but we choose the illustration of the combustion of those from a poker, in order to exemplify a fact in the "chemistry of every-day affairs," which proves that iron in a solid mass will not burn, but that when divided into small atoms it takes fire even more readily than many things which are considered easy to burn. It is just for the same

FIG. 9.

reason that Biddy prefers lighting a fire with chips rather than with a log of wood.

What a Glassful of Water will Hold.

It is generally thought that when a vessel is full of water, any solid substance immersed in it will cause it to overflow, and such will be the case if the substance is not soluble in the water; but the philosophic truth, that in dissolving a body, you do not increase the volume of the solvent, may be proved by a simple and interesting experiment. Saturate a certain quantity of water, at a moderate heat, with three ounces of sugar; and when it will no longer receive that, there is room in it for two ounces of salt of tartar, and after that for an ounce and a drachm of green vitriol, nearly six drachms of nitre, the same quantity of sal ammoniac, two drachms and a scruple of alum, and a drachm and a half of borax—when all these are dissolved in it, it will not have increased in volume.

We should observe that the salts used are to be "anhydrous;" that is, free from the water which they take up by crystallization. Nearly all salts can be rendered anhydrous by exposure to a high temperature which dries out the water.   It is interesting to observe that during this operation nearly all metallic salts lose their color; the sulphate of copper for instance is blue in its crystalline state, but becomes white when "anhydrous."

Another, although somewhat of a similar experiment, may be shown thus.   Fill a goblet with fine cotton wool, now take out the cotton and replace it with water "to the brim," then very gently let the cotton down into the water and it will be found that the glass will hold both water and cotton at the same time; thus it is twice full at one and the same time.

Observe: In this latter experiment, it is necessary to cleanse the cotton from the natural grease always adhering to it, by first boiling the cotton in an alkaline ley, such as soda or potash in water, then drying it and combing it out into its snowy form again.

To Raise up a Heavy Metal Mortar, or the like, with a Wine Glass.

Having inverted the mortar, spread on its bottom, or at least where the brim of the glass is to be placed, a little paste of flour and water.   Then pour some spirits of wine into a small cup, set fire to it, and hold the glass over it, so that the flame shall ascend into the glass, and heat and dilate the air within.   When the air is sufficiently dilated, place the glass without delay on the paste and press it tight against the bottom of the mortar, so that no air can pass in from without. Let it remain thus till the air within the glass is cooled; and then, if you lift up the glass, it will raise the mortar with it. You may use a piece of wet leather instead of the paste; but the latter is preferable, because the brims of common glasses are not always sufficiently level to press close to leather in every part, and a heated glass will be apt to crack when it comes in contact with wet leather.

Magic Milk.

Lime water is quite transparent, and clear as common spring water, but if we breathe or blow into it, the bright liquid becomes opalescent and as white as milk. The best way to try this simple experiment, is to put some powdered quick-lime into a wine bottle full of cold water; shake them well together now and then for a day; then allow the bottle to remain quiet till the next day, when

FIG. 10.

the clear lime-water may be poured off from the sediment. Now fill a wine-glass or tumbler with the lime water thus made, and

3*

blow through the liquid with a glass tube, a piece of new tobacco-pipe, or a clean straw, and in the course of a minute or so, as the magicians say, "the water will be turned into milk." By means of this *pastime*, "Wise Men" can ascertain which young ladies are in love and which young gentlemen are not. With a shrewd guess they present, as a test, a glass of lime water to the one, and of pure water to the other, with unerring effect.

The Inverted Glass of Water.

This little experiment affords at the same time amusement and instruction. Wipe a wine-glass perfectly dry, then pour water into it until it is full; indeed, if care be taken to have the glass quite bright, it may be filled above the brim. Now take a card, carefully place it on the top of the water, and press it on the rim of the glass. If this be cleverly done, there will be no air bubble between the card and the water; and if the glass be more than full, this can be with certainty accomplished. Now dexterously turn the glass upside down, keeping the finger on the card the while. This being done, the finger can be removed from the card, and yet the water will not run out, nor will the card fall away. The instructive part of this experiment consists in explaining why

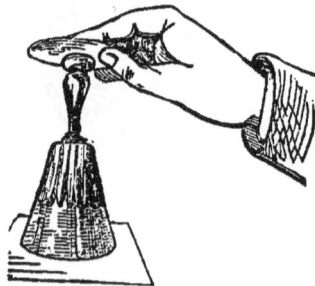

Fig. 11.

the water remains in the glass, which is this :—The familiar gurgling sound, when liquids are poured from a bottle, arises from the air rushing through the liquid, and taking its place in the bottle.

The air which passes into the bottle must be the same in bulk as the fluid which runs out, otherwise there will be no flow; and for the same reason we make a vent-peg hole in a cask; the law of nature demanding a pint of air for every pint of beer that is drawn. In the little experiment under illustration no air can get into the glass, and, as a consequence, no water can run out. If the glass, still inverted, be placed on to a tray, the card can be slipped away, and yet no water will flow out. In this way you can hand a glass of water to a friend, but he cannot remove it without spilling the whole.

The Balanced Coin.

This engraving represents what seems to be an astounding state-ment, namely, that a quarter or other piece of money can be made to spin on the point of a needle. To perform this experiment pro-cure a bottle, cork it, and in the cork place a needle. Now take

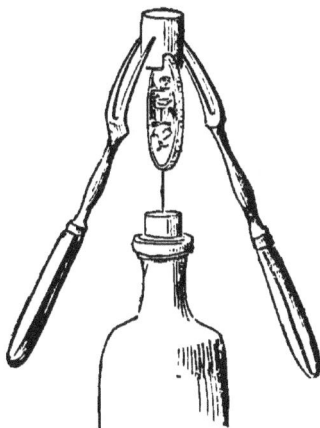

FIG. 12.

another cork and cut a slit in it so that the edge of the coin will fit into the slit; next place two forks in the cork, as seen in the engraving, and placing the edge of the coin on the needle, it will spin round without falling off. The reason is this, that the weight

of the forks, projecting as they do so much below the coin, brings
the centre of gravity of the arrangement much below the point of
suspension or the point of the needle, and therefore the coin
remains perfectly safe and upright.

The Magic Coffee-Pot.

Although the atmosphere may seem to us almost destitute of
weight, compared with the solid and liquid bodies of which the
earth is mainly composed, it nevertheless possesses actual weight,
and, like all other gases, exerts its pressure in all directions alike.
It is in this respect especially that gases differ from solids and
liquids, for the latter have only a tendency to press downwards,
while gases in general, from their extreme elasticity and the mo-
bility of their particles, press as much in an upward as in a downward direction.

If it were not for this circumstance, any soft object on the earth
would be completely crushed by the weight of the surrounding
air · for it is found that the atmosphere presses with a weight of

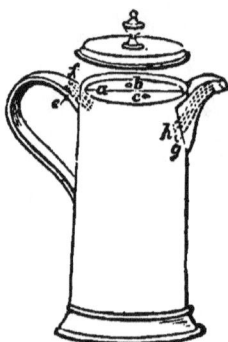

FIG. 13.

nearly 15 lbs. on every square inch of all objects on the earth's
surface; a weight which would be sufficient to overwhelm most of
the works of nature, if there were not a corresponding pressure in an
exactly opposite direction to counteract its effect. Such being the

case, it will be readily understood why a tube, open at one end and sealed at the other, may be filled with water, and inverted with the open end downwards, without the liquid escaping. The *upward* pressure of the air (not being counteracted by any *downward* pressure) acts upon the under surface of the water, thus opposing the natural tendency of the liquid to fall, and causing it to retain its position ; but if a hole be made in the sealed or upper end, the *upward* pressure of the atmosphere on the *under* surface will be counteracted by the *downward* pressure on the *upper* surface (which has now free access to the air), and the water will fall by its own weight.

The principle and action of the Magic Coffee-Pot will now be clearly comprehended. The pot is divided into two compartments, *b, c*, each of which has a pipe (*h g*) connected with the spout, and another leading through the hollow handle to the two little openings, *e, f*. Thus each compartment has two independent openings. The pot being uncovered, coffee is poured through *b* into the one compartment, and milk through *c* into the other, and the corks and lid are replaced. Now, if the thumb be placed upon the two openings, *e, f*, neither coffee nor milk will be able to be poured out ; for the pressure of the atmosphere at the spout is not counteracted, and therefore keeps both liquids in their respective compartments; but if the thumb be skilfully withdrawn from the aperture *f* and retained on the opening *e*, coffee will obviously escape from the spout on tilting the pot ; if, however, *f* be kept closed, and *e* opened, the milk will escape, and if the thumb be removed from both apertures, the milk and coffee will issue from the spout together. The effect of this trick is very startling, for the Coffee-Pot, which at first appears to be empty, may be made to discharge coffee, milk, or coffee and milk together at the pleasure of the company.

The Gong Poker

Tie a piece of string, about the substance of whipcord, round the handle of a poker, leaving the two ends about a foot long. Now take the ends of the cord, and pass them one over each ball of the thumb, so that the poker can be lifted up and suspended between

FIG. 14.

the hands. In this position place the thumbs and ends of the cord as close into each ear as convenient. If now a second person strike the poker, the one who holds it will hear a sound very surprising when experienced for the first time, but scarcely audible to the striker. If the blow be a sharp one, and struck with a hard body, as the back of a knife, the sound will be as strong as the deepest note of a piano, and if a hard blow with a hammer the sound will appear as powerful and booming as a cathedral bell. If the experiment be made with a large kitchen poker, then the sound is "stunning," and equals anything that can vibrate from the City Hall bell.

To place Water in a Drinking-Glass upside down.

Experiments of this kind are not only amusing, but instructive : they illustrate what at first sight appears to be "the laws of Nature reversed," while, in truth, when we are familiar with them, they teach the "immutability of Nature's laws." The more experiments a boy makes the greater number of rounds will he ascend up the "Ladder of Learning;" and when he is at the top, how bright is the prospect before him! All is beautiful, wonderful, and lovely. Then can he come down, and

> "Find tongues in trees, books in the running brooks,
> Sermons in stones, and good in everything."

But to our paradox. Procure a plate, a tumbler, and a small piece of tissue or silver paper. Set the plate on a table, and pour water in it up to the first rim. Now very slightly crumple up the paper, and place it in the glass; then set it on fire. When it is burnt out, or rather just as the last flame disappears, turn the glass quickly upside down into the water. Astonishing! the water rushes with great violence into the glass! Now you are satisfied that water can be placed in a drinking glass upside down. Hold the glass firm, and the plate also. You can now reverse the position of the plate and glass, and thus convince the most sceptical of the truth of your pneumatic experiment. Instead of burning paper, a little brandy or spirits of wine can be ignited in the glass; the result of its combustion being invisible, the experiment is cleaner.

FIG. 15.

The Revolving Image.

This little figure may be made to balance itself amusingly. Get a piece of wood, about two inches long; cut one end of it into the form of a man's head and shoulders, and let the other end taper off to a fine point. Next, furnish the little gentleman with a pair of wafters, shaped like oars, instead of arms; but they must be more than double the length of his body; stick them in his shoulders, and he is complete. When you place him on the tip of your finger, if you have taken care to make the point exactly

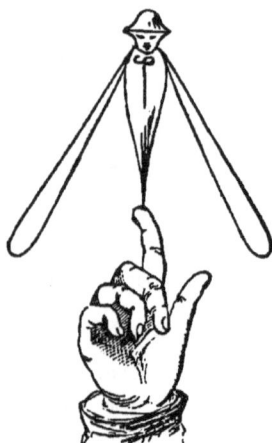

FIG. 16.

in the centre, he will stand upright, as seen in the engraving. By blowing on the wafters he may be made to turn round very quickly. It is explained by the reasons that were given in the experiment of the "Balanced Coin."

Fire by Percussion.

Take a hollow cylinder, somewhat like the common syringe, of some bad conductor of heat—of wood or of thick glass—but with this difference, that, instead of one end having an orifice for the ejection of liquid, it must be perfectly closed; it must have a piston like the syringe, also a bad conductor of heat, and which must be made to move in the cylinder perfectly air-tight. Place a bit of tinder of amadou impregnated with a little nitre—that is, steeped in a solution of saltpetre in water, and then dried—in the cylinder, then place the piston at the cylinder's mouth, and with a sudden and powerful thrust condense the air in the cylinder: the tinder may thus be made to ignite.

To put a lighted Candle under Water without extinguishing it.

Procure a good-sized cork or bung; upon this place a small lighted taper; then set it afloat in a pail of water. Now, with a steady hand invert a large drinking-glass over the light, and push it carefully down into the water. The glass being full of air, prevents the water entering it. You may thus see the candle burn *under* water, and bring it up again to the surface still alight. This experiment, simple as it is, serves to elucidate that useful contrivance called the diving-bell, being performed on the same principle.

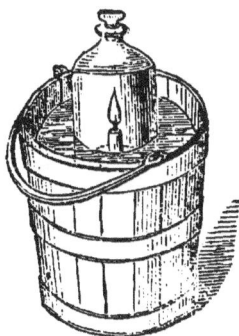

FIG. 17.

The largest drinking-glass holds but half a pint, so that your diving-light soon goes out for the want of air. As an average, a burning candle consumes as much air as a man, and he requires nearly a gallon of air every minute, so that according to the size of the glass over the flame you can calculate how many seconds it will remain alight; of course a large flame requires more air than a small one. For this and several other experiments a quart bell-glass is very useful, but being expensive they are not found in every parlor laboratory; one is, however, easily made from a green glass pickle bottle: get a glazier to cut off the bottom, and you have a bell-glass that Chilton would not reject.

The Immovable Card.

Take an ordinary visiting card and bend down the ends as represented in the annexed figure, then ask any person to blow it over.

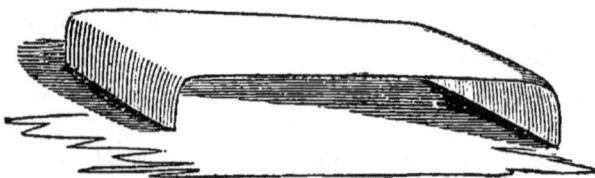

FIG. 18.

This seems easy enough, but it may be tried for hours without succeeding. It is, however, to be done by blowing sharply on the table at some distance from the card.

An Amusing Recreation.

The possibility of putting a bulk so large as twenty quarters, weighing four ounces, into a wine-glass already full to the brim with water, may be doubted ; yet, with a steady hand, it may be thus accomplished. First, procure a wine-glass, wipe it perfectly dry inside and out, especially round the rim ; pour the water gently into it from a spouted mug until the glass is full to the brim ; then drop the quarters edgeways gently in. Immediately the edge of the quarter touches the water, let it fall. Be careful not to wet the edges of the glass. Spring water answers better than soft. Having completed your task, you will observe, with surprise, how very much the water now stands above the level of the brim without flowing over ; this is caused by the " cohesive attraction" of the water being greater than the " attraction of gravity."

Inexplicable Motion and Sound.

Procure a piece of lead pipe, about two inches in the bore, and three inches long ; the thicker the lead is the better for the experiment. The pipe being set up on end, we will call it the stand. Next obtain a piece of brass, about eight inches long, one

FIG. 19.

to one inch and a half wide, and a quarter of an inch thick; file away the edges of one of the flat sides, to make it oval-shape, so that it will rock to and fro, if it be put in motion upon a table. Instead of having the brass filed, a blacksmith can give it a slight curve (observe, it must be lengthways) by a few blows with a sledge hammer; either way answers the purpose, and, when made, it is called a hummer. The dimensions here given are not essential to the success of the experiment; they are merely given as a guide. Now if one end of the hummer be made hot (not quite red hot) in a clear fire, and then laid across the stand, oval side downwards, giving it a slight rock to commence with, it will continue in motion, producing at the same time a peculiar humming sound, which motion and sound will continue for a very long time; in fact, until the stand and hummer are of the same temperature. The explanation of these phenomena must be solved by a genius as yet unknown.

Curious Effects of Oil upon Water, and Water upon Oil.

Fasten a piece of packthread round a tumbler, with strings of the same from each side, meeting above it in a knot at about a foot distance from the top of the tumbler. Then putting in as much water as will fill about one-third part of the tumbler, lift it up by the knot, and swing it to and fro in the air; the water will keep its place as steadily in the glass as if it were ice. But pour gently in upon the water about as much oil, and then again swing it in the air as before, the tranquillity before possessed by the water will be transferred to the surface of the oil, and the water under it will be violently agitated.

Another Curious Experiment with Oil and Water.

Drop a small quantity of oil into water agitated by the wind; it will immediately spread itself with surprising swiftness upon the surface, and the oil, though scarcely more than a teaspoonful, will produce an instant calm over a space several yards square. It should be done on the windward side of the pond or river, and you will observe it extend to the size of nearly half an acre, making it appear as smooth as a looking-glass. One remarkable circumstance in this experiment is the sudden, wide, and forcible spreading of a drop of oil on the surface of the water; for if a drop of oil be put upon a highly polished marble table, or a looking-glass laid horizontally, the drop remains in its place, spreading very little; but when dropped on water, it spreads instantly many feet round, becoming so thin as to produce the prismatic colors for a considerable space, and beyond them, so much thinner as to be invisible, except in its effect in smoothing the waves at a much greater distance. It seems as if a repulsion of its particles took place as soon as it touched the water, and so strong as to act on other bodies swimming on the surface, as straw, leaves, chips, etc., forcing them to recede every way from the drop, as from a centre, leaving a large clear space.

The Mechanical Bucephalus.

The illustration of the horse furnishes a very good solution of a popular paradox in mechanics: Given, a body having a tendency to fall by its own weight; required, how to prevent it from falling by adding to it a weight on the same side on which it tends to fall. The engraving shows a horse, the centre of gravity of which

FIG. 20.

is somewhere about the middle of its body. It is evident, there-fore, that were it placed on its hinder legs on a table, *a*, the line of its *direction* or centre, would fall considerably beyond its base, and the horse would fall on the ground. But to prevent this, there is a stiff wire attached to a weight or bullet connected with the body of the horse, and by this means the horse prances on a table without falling off; so that the figure which was incapable of supporting itself is actually prevented from falling by adding a weight to its unsupported end. This seems almost impossible; but when we consider that, in order to have the desired effect, the wire must be bent, and the weight be further under the table than the horse's feet are on it, the mystery is solved, as it brings the total weight of bullet and horse in such a position, that the tendency is rather to make it stand up than to let it fall down.

Solid Steel will float on Water.

If the blade of a well-polished knife be dipped into a basin of cold water, the particles of each of these two bodies do not seem to come in contact with each other; for when the blade is taken out, the water slides off leaving the blade quite dry, as if it had previously been smeared with some greasy substance. In the same way, if a common sewing needle be laid horizontally on a glass of water, it will not sink, but forms a kind of trench on the surface, on which it lies and floats about. This proceeds from the little attraction which exists between the cold water and the polished steel. It is necessary that both the knife, in the former experiment, and also the needle, should be dry and clean; otherwise the effect will not be produced. The needle must be carefully placed on the surface.

A Mariner's Compass made on a Lady's Thimble.

A magnetic needle, very desirable to ascertain the presence of iron, is easily made, of the requisite delicacy, where a magnet is accessible. A bit of thin steel wire, or a long fine stocking needle,

FIG. 21.

having a quarter of an inch cut off at the point, is to be heated in the middle, that it may be slightly bent there; then while hot a bit of sealing-wax is to be attached to the centre, and the point which was cut off, being heated at the thick end, is to be fixed in the sealing-wax, so that the sharp end may serve as a pivot, descending about one-eighth of an inch below the centre, taking care that the ends of the needle fall enough below the pivot to keep it from overturning. It must now be magnetized, by sliding one end of a magnet, half-a-dozen or more times, from the centre to one end of the needle; and the other end, a similar number of times, from the centre of the needle to its other end. A small brass thimble (not capped with iron) will do for the support; the point of the pivot being placed in one of the indentations, near the centre of the top, when, if well balanced, it will turn until it settles north and south. If one side preponderate, it must be nipped until the balance be restored.

Magical Increase.

Take a large drinking glass of a conical form, that is, small at bottom and large at top; and, having put into it a quarter, fill it about half way up with water; then place a plate upon the top of the glass, and turn it quickly over, that the water may not escape. A piece of silver as large as half-a-dollar will immediately appear on the plate, and somewhat higher up, another piece of the size of a quarter.

The Balanced Turk.

A decanter or bottle is first obtained, and in its cork is placed a needle; on this is balanced a ball of wood, having a cork or wooden figure cut out, standing on the top, such as that seen in the picture. From the ball project two wires bent semicircularly, having at their extremities two bullets. If the little apparatus be made as we have shown, you can give the bullets a twist, and the whole will turn round on the needle, the figure standing upright all the while, and twist it about from side to side as much as you like, it will always regain its erect position. The two bullets, in this case, cause the centre of gravity to fall below the ball on which the figure is placed, and, in consequence, as the centre of gravity always assumes the lowest position, it cannot do so without making the figure stand erect, or, in other words, until the bullets themselves are equally balanced. Any boy may whittle one of these

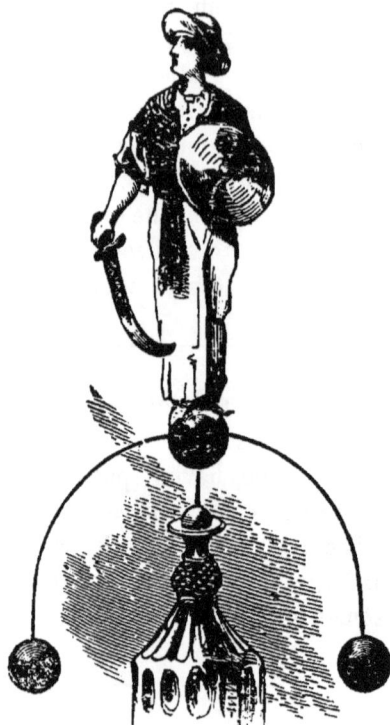

FIG. 22.

little toys out with a jack-knife, and cut any figure that may suit his fancy. To make a curious little variation of this experiment, drive a needle, head first, into the end of a cork; into each side of the cork stick a common fork; then invert a tumbler, and place the point of the needle on it, and give the cork a twirl with the fingers, when it will revolve for half an hour or more.

The Real Will-o'-the-Wisp.

Into a small retort place about an ounce of strong liquor of potash; that is, pure potash dissolved in water, together with about a drachm of phosphorus. Let the neck or beak of the retort dip into a saucer of water, say half an inch deep; now very gently heat the liquid in the retort with a spirit-lamp until it boils. In a few minutes the retort will be filled with a white cloud, then the gas generated will begin to bubble at the end of the saucer; a minute more, each bubble as it issues from the boiling fluid will *spontaneously take fire* as it comes into the air, forming at the

FIG. 23.

same time the philosopher's ring of phosphoric acid. Care is required in handling phosphorus; but our young chemical readers will, we think, not forego this wonderful experiment for the want of due attention, for, without proper care on their part, we must give up showing them wonders, even greater than these.

Curious Motions.

Procure a basin of milk-warm water, throw into it half-a-dozen pieces of camphor about the size of a pea; in a minute they will begin to move, and acquire a rotatory and progressive motion, which will continue for a considerable time. If now, one drop of oil of turpentine, or sweet oil, or even of gin (if allowed on the premises), be let fall upon the water, the pieces of camphor will dart away, and be deprived of their motion and vivacity. Little pieces of cork, that have been soaked in ether, act much in the same way as camphor, when thrown upon water.

Camphor, being highly combustible, will burn if ignited while floating upon water, producing a singular effect, reminding one of

4

the lamps which the Hindoo maidens cast upon the waters of the Ganges as mystic messengers to their distant lovers, or to their spirits after death.

The Man in the Moon.

This is glorious fun for the long evenings, and will be found a valuable addition to the amusements provided at evening parties. In a room with folding doors, which will be best suited to the purpose—or otherwise it must be suspended from the ceiling—strain a large sheet across the partition. In the front room place the company, who will remain in comparative darkness, and in the back room put a bright lamp or candle, with a looking-glass reflector, or a polished tin one if it be convenient, on the ground. When an individual stands between the light and the sheet, his reflection, magnified to immense proportions, will be thrown forward on the screen, and when he jumps over the light, it will appear to the spectators in front, as if he had jumped upwards through the ceiling. Some amusing scenes may be thus contrived with a little ingenuity. Chairs and tables may be called down from above simply by passing them across the light; a struggle between two seeming combatants may take place, and one be seen to throw the other up in the air on the same principle. A game at cards, with pieces of cardboard cut out so as to represent the pips, may be played out, and beer poured from a jug into a glass, sawdust giving the best shadowy imitation of the fluid, may be imbibed during the game with great effect. Care should be taken to keep the profile on the screen as distinct as possible, and practice will soon suggest some highly humorous situations.

The Mimic Vesuvius.

This experiment is a demonstration of the heat and light which are evolved during chemical combination. The substance, phosphorus, has a great affinity for oxygen gas, and wherever it can

get it from it will, especially when aided by the application of heat.
To perform this experiment, put half a drachm of solid phosphorus
into a Florence-oil flask, holding the flask slantingly, that the phosphorus may not take fire and break the glass; pour upon it a gill
and a half of water, and place the whole over a tea-kettle lamp, or
any common lamp, filled with spirits of wine; light the wick, which
should be about half an inch from the flask; and as soon as the
water is boiling hot, streams of fire, resembling sky-rockets, will
burst at intervals from the water; some particles will also adhere
to the sides of the glass, immediately display brilliant rays, and
thus continue until the water begins to simmer, when a beautiful

FIG. 24.

imitation of the aurora borealis will commence, and gradually
ascend until this collects into a pointed cone at the mouth of the
flask; when this has continued for half a minute, blow out the
flame of the lamp, and the apex of fire that was formed at the
mouth of the flask, will rush down, forming beautiful illumined
clouds of fire, rolling over each other for some time, and when
these disappear, a splendid hemisphere of stars will present itself.
After waiting a minute or two, light the lamp again, and nearly
the same phenomena will be displayed as at the beginning. Let a
repetition of lighting and blowing out the lamp be made for three

or four times, so that the number of stars may be increased; and after the third or fourth act of blowing out the lamp, the internal surface of the flask will be dry. Many of the stars will shoot with great splendor from side to side, whilst others will appear and burst at the mouth of the flask. What liquid remains in the flask will serve for the same experiment three or four times, without adding any water. Care should be taken, after the operation is over, to put the flask in a cool and secure place.

The Revolving Syphon.

Take a tall, narrow, round vessel, A, and fit two pieces of wood, *a, a,* across the inside. Bore holes through the pieces, so that

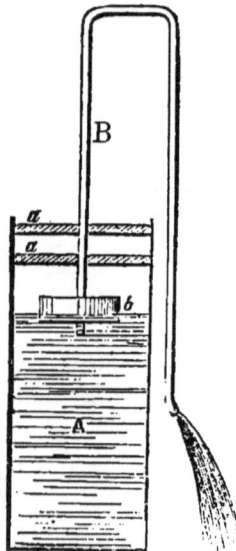

FIG. 25.

they will be in the centre of the vessel, and one above the other. Bend a small tube of any material which bends readily into a

be converted into an illuminating gas; and with this gas nearly all our cities are now lighted in the dark hours of night. To make it as represented in our engraving, obtain some coal dust (or walnut or butternut meats will answer), and fill the bowl of a pipe with it; then cement the top over with some clay, place the bowl in the fire, and soon smoke will be seen issuing from the end of the stem; when that has ceased coming, apply a light, and it will burn brilliantly for several minutes; after it has ceased, take the pipe from the fire and let it cool, then remove the clay, and a piece of coke will be found inside; this is the excess of carbon over the hydrogen contained in the coal, for all the hydrogen will combine with carbon at a high temperature, and make what are called hydro-carbons—a series of substances containing both these elemental forms of matter.

A Flying Toy.

As it may be an amusement to some of my readers to see a machine rise in the air by mechanical means, I will describe an

Fig. 27.

syphon, B, keeping the legs straight, with two right angles
top. Next turn the end of the longest outward, so that th
part will correspond with the line of a circle, the shortest leg
the centre. When the syphon is properly placed the bent
horizontal. Put the short leg loosely down through the h
the pieces, after which push it tightly half an inch through a
b, large enough to float and sustain the syphon. The lon
will now be on the outside of the vessel. Pour clean water
the vessel until the cork nearly touches the cross piece. Ch
the syphon by suction, and it will commence revolving rap
around the vessel, continuing as long as any water remains, p
vided the inner leg is long enough.

The Mimic Gas House.

The next illustration shows a simple way of making illuminatin
gas by means of a tobacco pipe. Bituminous coal contains a num

FIG. 26.

ber of chemical compounds, nearly all of which can, by distillation,

instrument of this kind, which any one can construct at the expense of ten minutes' labour :

a and *b* are two corks, into each of which are inserted four wing-feathers from any bird, so as to be slightly inclined, like the sails of a windmill, but in opposite directions to each set.   A round shaft is fixed in the cork *a*, which ends in a sharp point.   At the upper part of the cork *b* is fixed a whalebone bow, having a small pivot hole in its centre, to receive the point of the shaft.   The bow is then to be strung equally on each side to the upper portion of the shaft, and the little machine is completed.   Wind up the string by turning the bow, so that the spring of the bow may unwind the corks, with their anterior edges ascending; then place the cork, with the bow attached to it, upon a table, and with a finger pressed on the upper cork, press strongly enough to prevent the string from unwinding, and taking it away suddenly, the instrument will rise to the ceiling.

The Revolving Serpent.

This illustration represents an amusing and instructive experiment, which proves the ascension of heated air by rendering its

FIG. 28.   FIG. 29.

effects visible, and it may also be used to test the direction of the currents in our rooms and dwellings.   To construct one, a piece of card board is taken and cut in the form of a spiral, as at A, and to give effect it may be painted to represent a serpent. Then prepare a stand, as at B, having a needle in its upper end, and suspend the serpent from its centre on the needle, when it will assume the position shown at B. If this be now placed over a stove, or the tail of the serpent suspended by a bit of thread over a lamp, the heated air ascending through it will cause it to revolve in a very amusing manner. Two serpents may be made to turn in opposite directions, by pulling one out from the one side, and the other in the reverse direction, so that their heads may point towards each other when suspended.

The Ring Suspended by a Burnt Thread.

Put a teaspoonful of salt in a wineglassful of water; stir it up and place in it some coarse sewing cotton, such as Mamma calls No. 16; in about an hour take out the thread and dry it. Tie a piece of this prepared cotton to a small ring, about the size of a wedding-ring; hold it up, and set fire to the thread. When it has burnt out the ring will not fall, but remain suspended, to the astonishment of all beholders. Philosophers account for this effect by stating that the salt in the thread forms, with the ashes of the cotton, a fine film of glass, which is strong enough to support the ring, or any other small weight.

The Spanish Dancer.

The laws which govern the motion of bodies are capable of many pleasing illustrations, and the example which we now give of causing rotary motion is very interesting and easily performed.

Take a piece of card, and cut out a little figure like that in the engraving, and paste or gum it in an erect position on the inside of a watch-glass, A. Then procure a black japanned waiter, B, or a clean plate will do, and holding it in an inclined position, place the figure and watch glass on it, and they will, of course, slide down.   Next, let fall a drop of water on the waiter, place the watch-glass on it, and again incline the waiter, and instead of the watch-glass sliding down it will begin to revolve.   It will continue to

FIG. 30.

revolve with increasing velocity, obeying the inclination and posi-tion of the plane, as directed by the hand of the experimentalist. The reason of this is, in the first place, in consequence of the cohe-sion of the water to the two surfaces, a new force is introduced by which an unequal degree of resistance is imparted to different parts of the watch-glass in contact with the waiter, and consequently, in its effort to slide down, it revolves.   Again, if the drop of water be observed, it will be seen that it undergoes a change of figure ; a film of water by capillary action is drawn to the fore-most portion of the glass, while, by the centrifugal force, a body of water is thrown under the hinder part of it.   The effect of both of these actions is to accelerate the motion, or, in other words, to gradually increase the speed.

The Funny Funnel

This magic instrument consists of a small funnel, placed in a larger one, and united to it only at the top, thus forming an open space, a, a, between the two.

The handle being held in one hand, and the opening, c, being

4*

stopped by a finger of the other hand, the funnel is completely
filled with water, so as to allow the liquid to flow over from the
interior into the space, *a, a*.   The thumb is then placed upon the
aperture *b*, and the finger withdrawn from *c*, when all the water in
the inner part will, of course, run out, but the liquid contained in
the outer compartment, *a, a*, will be retained by the pressure of the
atmosphere at *c*, which is not counterbalanced by any corresponding
pressure at the upper surface.

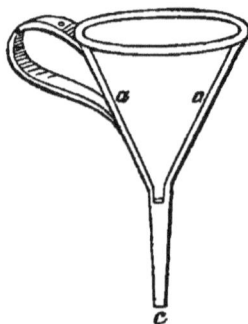

Fig. 31.

However, immediately the thumb is removed from the aperture
b, the air will enter it and find its way into the compartment, and
the pressure being thus counterbalanced, the water will all be dis-
charged from it.   It will thus seem as if the fresh supply is derived
from some magic or invisible source.   In showing a trick with it
we induce one of the company to drink out of the funnel, and then
cause the liquid to flow out of his elbow or his ear, to the great
delight of all the boys and girls in the room.

Manner of Melting Steel, and Seeing it Liquify.

You will first make a piece of steel red-hot, in the fire ; then
take it up with a pair of pincers, and in the other hand hold a
stick of sulphur, which you apply to the steel.   As soon as they
touch each other, you will see the steel flow as if it were a liquid.

A Trick by Means of which you Change the Color of the Plumage of a Bird, or the Petal of a Flower.

To effect this metamorphosis, you must have jars or earthen vases with narrow rims near their mouths; these vases should be large enough to contain the bird you mean to put in, suspended from the opening by the neck. You will require, also, large corks or bungs, which will fit the mouth of the vase. To perform this experiment on any kind of bird you will begin by making a hole in the cork large enough to hold the neck of the bird, without strangling it. You will then divide the cork into two parts, so that each piece has in it one-half the circular hole: you will thus be able easily to place it round the bird's neck without running the risk of injuring the creature. Do this, and then put in the bottom of the vase one ounce of quick-lime, and on it two drachms of sal ammoniac. When you see the effervescence begin to take place, put in the bird, letting the cork which is round its neck fit tightly in the neck of the vase. The plumage exposed to the vapor of this effervescence will become impregnated with different colors produced by the combination. Withdraw the cork, and the bird, as soon as you perceive that its feathers are turning different colors, which will be in the course of two or three minutes; you will run the risk of suffocating the bird if you expose it to the fumes for a longer period.

In changing the tints of a flower you need only draw the stem through a hole in the cork, so as to keep it suspended in the vase for two or three minutes, which, in this case as well as in the preceding, will suffice.

Observe, that although earthen jars are spoken of, those made of glass have evidently the advantage, as you can see the process, and ascertain its progress.

A Magic Picture, representing alternately Summer and Winter.

Draw on cardboard a landscape scene, in which the ground, the trunks of the trees, and the branches, are painted with the ordinary colors, and in such as are appropriate to the subject; but draw and wash over the grass and the foliage with the liquid which we shall describe. You will then have a picture which, in the ordinary temperature of the air, will present the aspect of a country during the winter, when trees and earth are deprived of their verdure. Warm it sufficiently, but not too much, and you see it covered with leaves and herbage, as in spring.

The liquid for producing this effect :

Take some zaffer, that is, metallic earth of cobalt, which gives the blue color to zaffer, and which may be obtained at any drug store, and digest it in aqua regia. Dilute this mixture, which is highly caustic, with pure water, and use it to paint the verdure of your picture. It will be invisible until warmed, when all the parts you may have touched with this preparation will be green.

A Color which you can cause to Appear and Disappear.

Take a glass bottle : put into it some volatile alkali, in which you have dissolved copper filings. This will produce a blue liquid. Present the bottle to some one to cork, jesting a little with him, and to the great surprise of the company, it will be observed that the color disappears as soon as the cork is put in. You easily make it reappear by uncorking the bottle, which does not seem the least surprising part of the matter.

The Magic Portrait.

Take a glass, such as is generally used to cover a portrait or hair devices in a bracelet, and which is always slightly concave, and another piece of the same size, but of ordinary glass, and as thin as possible ; cover the concave side of the first with a composition made of lard and a *very* little white wax, mixed together. Fasten the two glasses very exactly, the one over the other, so that this composition is between them ; and join them by binding the edges together with a bit of bladder, fastened with isinglass. Let it get perfectly dry ; and after having cleaned the glasses well, put a portrait, or any other picture you please, under the flat side. Afterwards have it put into a frame, which will entirely conceal the binding of the edges.

EXPERIMENT.

When you warm the picture a little, the composition you have introduced between the two glasses becoming liquid, is also rendered entirely transparent, and you perceive the subject of the picture with perfect clearness. Otherwise, it conceals the portrait, just as if there were a piece of white paper under the glass. It will appear and disappear as often as you choose, on making it warm, or letting it get cold.

To Draw two Figures with Charcoal on a Wall, so that one will Light a Taper, and the other Extinguish it.

You draw two figures with charcoal on the wall: any you please, but the head of an old man and woman are among the most appropriate. At the mouth of one you put a little gunpowder, which you fasten on with isinglass; at the mouth of the other, a morsel of phosphorus, fastened in the same way. When you take a lighted taper near the mouth that has the gunpowder, the explosion extinguishes it; then taking it near the phosphorus it lights itself again.

A Vessel that will let Water out at the Bottom, as soon as the Mouth is uncorked.

Provide a tin vessel, two or three inches in diameter, and five or six inches in height, having a mouth about three inches in width; and in the bottom several small holes, just large enough to admit a small needle. Plunge it in water with its mouth open, and when full, while it remains in the water, stop it very closely. You can play a trick with a person, by desiring him to uncork it; if he places it on his knee for that purpose, the moment it is uncorked the water will run through at the bottom, and make him completely wet.

PART III.

MISCELLANEOUS TRICKS, A CURIOUS COLLECTION
OF ENTERTAINING EXPERIMENTS, AMUSING PUZ-
ZLES, QUEER SLEIGHTS, RECREATIONS IN ARITH-
METIC, AND FIRESIDE GAMES FOR FAMILY PAS-
TIME.

The Magic Purse.

With a piece of morocco, or any other suitable material, let a
purse be constructed similar to the one given here. The puzzle is
to open the same without removing any of the rings.

Fig. 32.

Pass loop *a* up through ring No. 2 and over No. 1, then pass
loop *b* over rings 1 and 2 up through No. 2, and over No. 1, as
before; when the same may be easily drawn through rings 3, 4, 5.

Again pass loop *c* through ring No. 7 over 8, draw it up through ring 6, and the purse is complete.

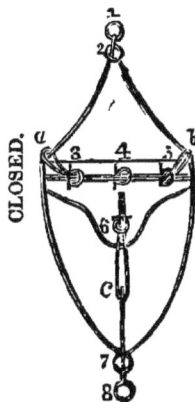
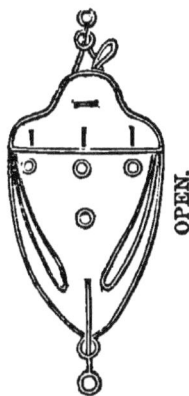

FIG. 33.   FIG. 34.

To Place Seven Counters upon an Eight-Pointed Star.

Draw a star with eight points (see Fig. 35), which points are connected together by the lines A D, D G, G B, B E, E H, H C, C F, F A. Provide yourself with eight counters, numbered from

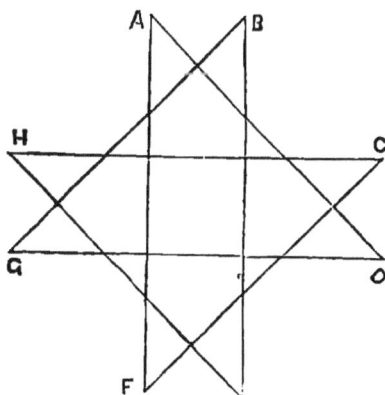

FIG. 35.

1 to 8. With these the points of the star are to be covered, and in the following manner : Commence by placing a counter upon

any uncovered point of the star, push it along the line which unites it to the opposite point, and leave it lying there. You must proceed in this way with the seven counters, when you place the eighth upon the remaining uncovered point, which makes the star complete.

This feat, although a merely mechanical one, cannot be effected, unless the person attempting it proceeds in the following order :

The first counter you place, say upon point A, move it to the point F, and leave it there. The second counter you place upon the point D, move it to A, and leave it there. The third you place upon G, move it to D, and leave it ; the fourth you place upon B, and move it to G ; the fifth upon E, and move it to B ; the sixth upon H, and move it to E ; the seventh upon C, and move it to H ; and, finally, place the eighth counter upon C, when every point of the star will be covered. The solution lies simply in these words, " Always slide one to the last point you started from." Thus, if you begin at F, and slide one to A, send one to A, and so on, till you have got the whole of them on.

The Twelve-cornered Arithmetical Star.

The circle, Fig. 36, is divided at the twelve points A, B, C, D, E, F, G, H, I, K, L, M, by lines so drawn that they form a star with twelve points. From the point A, draw a line to F, from F to L, to D, to I, to B, to G, to M, to E, to K, to C, to H, and back again to A.

The problem now to be solved, is how to distribute the twelve numbers of the following arithmetical progression 2, 4, 6, 8, 10, 12, 14, 16, 18, 20, 22, 24, into the twelve compartments of the twelve letters which stand at the twelve points of the star in such a manner, that the sum of any two numbers that lie side by side, when added together, shall be equal to the sum of the two numbers which are at the two opposite points of the star.

This singular arrangement of the numbers is effected in the following manner : Place number 2 over the ring which incloses

the letter A, 4 over F, 6 over L, 8 over D, 10 over I, and so on
and the numbers will then be distributed as appears in Fig. 36.

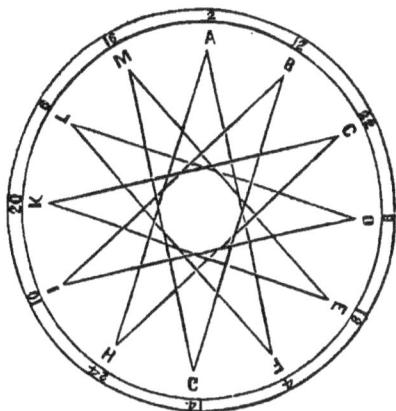

FIG. 36.

You may now take any two numbers that lie side by side, and
add them together, and their sum will always be equal to the sum
of the two numbers found at the opposite points of the star.

For example, the sum of the two numbers 14 and 4 which
cover the letters G and F, is 18, and so also is the sum of the
numbers 16 and 2, which are placed over the opposite letters M
and A. The same is the case with every other pair of numbers
and their opposites.

The Secret of Clairvoyance or Second Sight.

The art of telling the name of an article, the number on a bank-
note, the color of a substance, the name of a metal, the value of
a piece of money, the nature of a precious stone, and other things,
by a person whose eyes are blindfolded, has been called *Clairvoyance, Second-Sight, or Double-Sight.*

The "Mysterious Lady," Robert Heller, and other persons pre-
tending to this apparent faculty, have, from time to time, appeared
before the public for the above purpose, causing a degree of asto-

nishment in the minds of the audience almost without parallel; hence these exhibitions have been denominated "Magic," a name which implies an effect without a known cause. By a known cause we mean that which is patent to the world, and not to the individual.

From the time when the Oracles of Delphos were consulted to our own day, man has invented things to astonish his brethren; and until the secret of one has been explained, and another invented, these mysteries have continued.

Before science was made a branch of polite learning magic had full sway, and was believed to be a gift from the Spirit of Evil to those men who paid tribute to his Satanic Majesty. Happily for the present age superstition has passed away, and we are no longer horrified by hearing that a " learned judge " has ignorantly condemned such and such a person to be burned for witchcraft, which, unfortunately for the many poor creatures who suffered, was the case in the time of " good Queen Elizabeth," and even at a more recent period, at Salem.

Clairvoyance, like all the presumed magical arts, astonishes people no more when it is explained to them. They are then surprised at their own dulness and incapacity " to see through" such a simple thing.

The whole system of presumed "double-sight" rests with two persons—one who advances to the audience *to receive* the article desired to be experimented upon, and who *asks a question* of the other; and the blindfolded person, *who replies*. The effect of these questions and answers being arranged into a system and order, constitutes the whole art of clairvoyance.

Every question has a corresponding answer; and, to be perfect, requires a good memory—not more, however, perhaps, than that required of an actor who learns "a part" in a new tragedy. The simplicity of the questions principally misleads the audience, being no other than an ordinary interrogation which any one would make; modified only by an understanding between the confederate parties, that the same sentence, differently arranged or put, calls forth a different reply, thus :—

Question. Is it plain or ornamented?
Answer. Ornamented.
Question. Is it ornamented or plain?
Answer. Plain.

We will now give a few illustrations of the system of questions and answers, premising that the same order can be, and is frequently, carried out to a very elaborate extent. First, then, we have questions relating to colors, precious stones, metals, wearing apparel, jewellery, numbers and dates, money, miscellaneous articles, etc., etc.

FOR COLOR.

Question. What color is it?—*Answer.* Black.
Q. What is the color?—A. Blue.
Q. Tell me the color?—A. Green.
Q. Has it a color?—A. White.
Q. Any color?—A. Orange or yellow.
Q. Name the color?—A. Brown.

FOR METALS.

Q. What metal?—A. Gold.
Q. What is the metal?—A. Silver.
Q. Tell me the metal?—A. Copper.
Q. Name the metal?—A. Iron or steel.
Q. What metal is it?—A. Brass.

FOR STONES.

Q. What stone is it?—A. Jet.
Q. What is the stone?—A. Topaz.
Q. Tell me the stone?—A. Emerald.
Q. Name the stone?—A. Diamond.
Q. Do you know the stone?—A. Cornelian.
Q. Any stone?—A. Amethyst.

MISCELLANEOUS ARTICLES.

Q. What have I here?—A. A purse.
Q. What is this?—A. A toothpick.

Question. Name this.—*A.* A pocket-comb.

   Q. This will puzzle you.—*A.* Court-plaster.

   Q. Speak loud.—*A.* A letter.

   Q. Answer instantly.—*A.* A handkerchief.

   Q. Has it a color ?—*A.* White.

   Q. Is it perfumed ?—*A.* Yes.

   Q. Tell me now.—*A.* Keys.

   Q. Is this of any use ?—*A.* An almanack.

   Q. What should be done with this?—*A.* Burn it; **a** cigar, or cigar-case.

   Q. Do ladies or gentlemen use this?—*A.* Ladies; **a** needle-case or pincushion.

   Q. Do you know this?—*A.* Yes—well I remember it— a cane or walking-stick.

   Q. Now can you tell ?—*A.* A pocket-book.

   Q. Is this for any purpose ?—*A.* A reticule.

   Q. How do you tell what I possess ?—*A.* By a sympathy—a ring.

ARTICLES OF JEWELLERY.

   Q. Would you like this ?—*A.* Yes ; a watch.

   Q. Do you admire this ?—*A.* A brooch.

   Q. Who gave me this ?—*A.* A lady—a bracelet.

   Q. What is now in my hand ?—*A.* A breast-pin.

   Q. Now, who gave this?—*A.* A gentleman—a chain.

   Q. Tell me, instantly, who gave this ?—*A.* A lady—a chain.

MONEY.

   Q. What have I now ?—*A.* Money.

   Q. Now what have I got?—*A.* An eagle.

   Q. Can you tell again ?—*A.* Half-a-dollar.

   Q. Is this the same ?— *A.* A dime.

   Q. You say I have money, but don't tell me the coin.— *A.* A florin.

   Q. You say I have money; why not tell me the value, if you can see it ?—*A.* Half an eagle.

   Q. I cannot hear you.—*A.* A bank-note.

Question. What is its value?—*A.* Five dollars.

Q. Of what value is it?—*A.* Ten dollars.

Q. Can you tell its value?—*A.* Twenty dollars.

Q. How much is it worth?—*A.* Fifty dollars.

The above illustrations are sufficient to show the plan of simple questions; but as it frequently happens that *particulars* of the articles are required, they then become complex, but are no less easily understood than the simple questions, because the latter are only combinations of the former. Thus,—

AN ARTICLE DESCRIBED.

Q. 1. Is this for any purpose?—*A.* A reticule.

Q. 2. What color is it?—*A.* Black.

Q. 3. What have I here?—*A.* A purse.

Q. 4. Tell me the color?—*A.* Green.

Q. 5. What have I now?—*A.* Money.

Q. 6. I cannot hear you.—*A.* Bank-note.

Q. 7. Of what value is it?—*A.* Ten dollars.

Q. 8. Is this the same?—*A.* No : a dime.

Q. 9. Tell me now?—*A.* Keys.

Q. 10. Answer instantly?—*A.* A handkerchief.

It should be understood that the questioner, during the process of eliciting the answers, uses such actions as are necessary to call forth the replies. After the second question is answered, the reticule is opened, and the purse (if any) taken out; the purse is also opened, and the note or dollar (as the case may be) is brought forth. These being returned to the bag, the keys or handkerchief are removed before the ninth or tenth question is put.

ANOTHER ARTICLE DESCRIBED.

Q. Would you like this?—*A.* A watch.

Q. What is the metal?—*A.* Silver.

Q. Now who gave this?—*A.* A gentleman; there is a chain attached.

Q. Of what metal is the chain made?—*A.* Gold.

OTHER ARTICLES DESCRIBED.

Question. Do you admire this?—*A.* Yes, a brooch.

   Q. Do you know the stone ?—*A.* Yes, cornelian.

   Q. Has it a color ?—*A.* White.

   Q. Now can you tell ?—*A.* A pocket-book.

   Q. What is the color of the leather ?—*A.* Blue.

   Q. Speak loud ! (here the book is opened)—*A.* A letter.

   Q. The wax—" what color is it" sealed with ?—*A.* Black.

We have now given sufficient explanation and illustrations to show the basis of this system. Those who wish to practise it must invent a vocabulary of their own, or make such additions as are necessary to render it complete. The most numerous or various questions are required for the " Miscellaneous" articles expected to be met with in a large party; but we doubt not that many of our readers will readily accomplish the task; and, when learnt, it will afford much amusement to themselves and friends.

The Oval Puzzle.

With a piece of stiff paper or cardboard, form a complete circle; cut the same into eight parts, and with them produce two perfect ovals; the figures, large or small, should be in proportion to those given below.

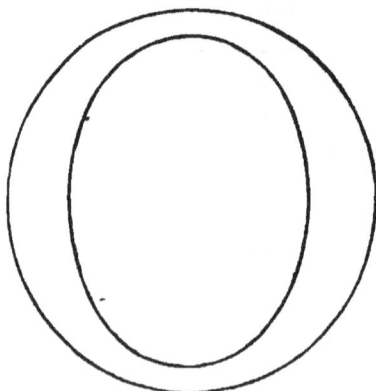
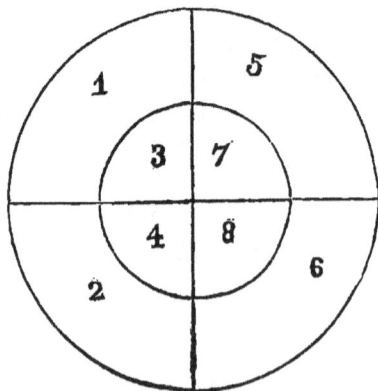

      Fig. 37.   Fig. 38.

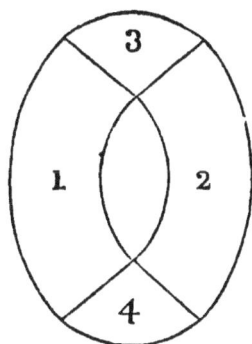 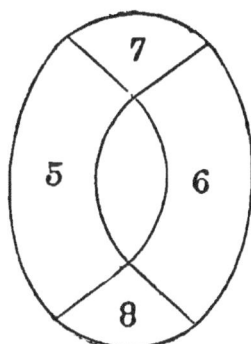

FIG. 39.   FIG. 40.

Cut the card as in Fig. 38, and you then can easily form the Figs. 281 and 282.

The Magical Arrangement.

Arrange the following twelve counters, so that instead of counting four counters in a row, they will count five in a row.

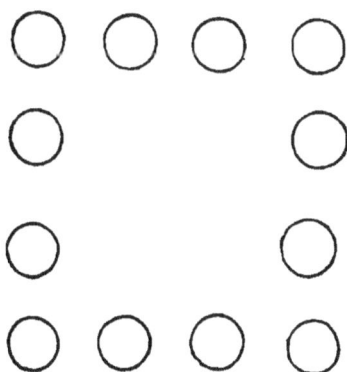

FIG. 41.

Have three at each side, and double counters at the corners.

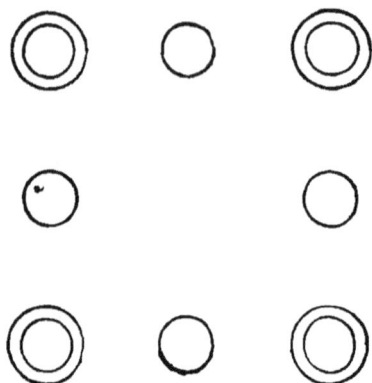

FIG. 42.

How to Cut a Visiting Card for a Cat to Jump through it.

Cut the card through the centre, leaving a perfect bar at each end; then proceed by cutting the card according to the lines indicated in the subjoined engraving, taking care that you do **not** cut

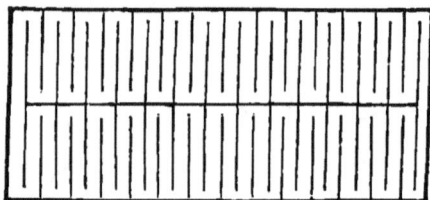

FIG. 43.

through and thus separate the links. When the card has been thus carefully cut it may be drawn out to form a hoop for pussy to jump through, or it will make a pretty collar for her to wear.

The Board and Ball.

Get the cover of a small cigar box, or any other thin board, about five inches long, and cut it out the shape as represented in Fig.

44.   Then arrange the strings and balls as shown in the same engraving.

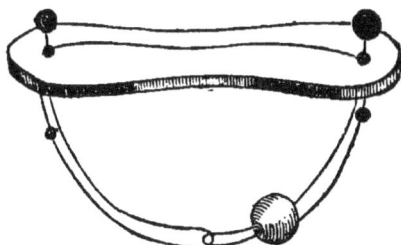

FIG. 44.

The trick is, to get the large ball off the string without untying it, or removing any of the smaller balls. Push the ball close up to the wood, and pull the loop of string down through as much as it will come; then pass the end of the loop through the hole in the wood and over the pellet as here shown. (Fig. 45.) The two loops will then separate, and the ball can easily be taken off.

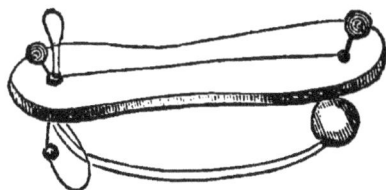

FIG. 45.

The knots beneath the wood prevent the loops being pulled through by the pellets.

To Tell a Person any Number he may privately fix on.

When the person has fixed on any number (say six) bid him double it, and add four to the doubling; then multiply the whole by five; to the product let him add twelve, and multiply the amount by ten. From the total of all this let him deduct three hundred and twenty, and tell you the remainder, from which, if

5

you cut off the two last figures, the number that remains will be the one he fixed on.

Example.

6	16	92
2	5	10
12	80	920
4	12	320
16	92	6(00

The Cypher Puzzle.

The authenticity of Shakspeare's autograph being volubly discussed by a large and merry party assembled round the fireside of a cheerful country mansion, a young lady present, rejoicing in the possession of the bluest of blue eyes, and sunniest of golden hair, was heard to remark, "That of all things, she envied the possessor of such a treasure." On retiring to rest, she discovered the following *jeu d'esprit* on her dressing-table :

You 0 a 0
But I 0 thee ;
O, 0 no 0,
But, O 0 me.

And, O, let my 0
Thy 0 be :
And give 0 0
I 0 the.

ANSWER.

You sigh for a cypher,
But I sigh for thee ;
O, sigh for no cypher,
But, O sigh for me.

And, O, let my cypher
Thy cypher be :
And give sigh for sigh for
I sigh for thee.

The Remainder.

A very pleasing way to arrive at an arithmetical sum, without the use of either slate or pencil, is to ask a person to think of a figure, then to double it, then to add a certain figure to it, now halve the whole sum, and finally to subtract from that the figure first thought of. You are then to tell the thinker what is the remainder.

The key to this lock of figures is, that *half* of whatever sum you request to be added during the working of the sum *is the remainder.* In the example given five is the half of ten, the number requested to be added. Any amount may be added, but the operation is simplified by giving only even numbers, as they will divide without fractions.

Example.

Think of	7
Double it	=14
Add 10 to it	10
Halve it	½)24
Which will leave . . .	12
Subtract the number thought of .	7
THE REMAINDER will be . .	5

The Sphynx.

Let thirty straight lines be drawn in such a position so as to form a symmetrical figure, on each of these lines there shall be

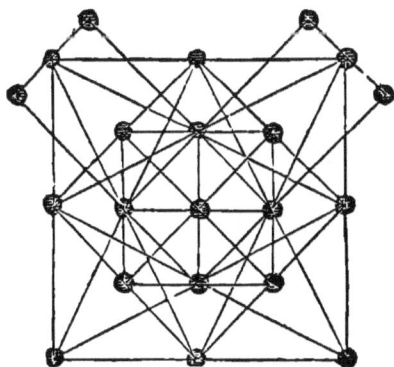

FIG. 46.

placed three black balls, or any other article the reader may suggest, bearing in mind that the whole number shall not exceed twenty-one. Required to know how this may be accomplished? They were arranged as represented in Fig. 46.

The Crowning Puzzle.

First place ten draught men in a row thus, 1, 2, 3, 4, 5, 6, 7, 8, 9, 10. Now the difficulty is to lift a man up, and passing over *two* each time, and no more, to crown the next to them, continuing thus until they are all kings. In passing over a king it is to be reckoned as two men; thus, for instance (not that this is any explanation of the puzzle, that is for our young friends to solve) suppose we place the 6th on the 3d, it must pass over two men; and then the 4th on the 2nd, we pass a king (two men); here will be two crowns effected, but the puzzle completed must have five crowns and no men. Remember well, that it is required to pass over two, but never more nor less than that number.

Explanation.—Place the 4th on the 1st, the 6th on the 9th, the 8th upon the 3d, the 2d on the 5th, and the 7th on the 10th.

The Carpenter Puzzled.

A ship having sprung a leak at sea, and being in great danger the carpenter could find nothing to mend it with, except a piece

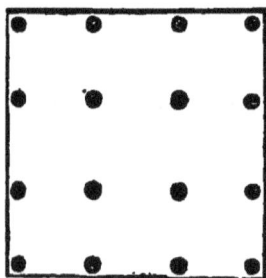
Fig. 47.

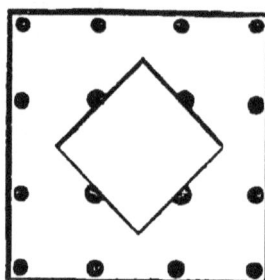
Fig. 48.

of wood, of which the annexed is a correct representation (Fig. 47), supposing the black dots in it to represent holes in the wood, thus apparently preventing him from cutting out of it the sized piece he wanted, which was exactly one quarter of the board. Required, the way in which he must cut this piece of wood, to obtain out of it a piece exactly one-fourth its own size having no holes in it.

An examination of Fig. 48 will show how the square piece was cut from the board.

The Magic Star.

Cut out of stiff white paper thirty-six small squares. Upon these you write 36 numbers, from one to thirty-six, and place them in six rows upon the table as follow :—

```
        B                           C
        32                         26
          33                     30
            31                 29
              11             24
                13         8
                  1     14
A 36 35 34 28 16 15  X  7 5 27 25 22 23 D
                  9     12
                10         2
              17             21
            6                 18
          3                     4
        19                         20
        F                           E
```

FIG. 49.

After the six rows, A X, B X, C X, D X, E X, and F X, are laid upon the table, you choose six persons out of the company, A, B, C, D, E, F, and request the first person, A, to choose any number out of the row of numbers marked A X, and to keep it in mind. You request the second person, B, to choose a number out of the row B X, and the third person out of the row C X, the fourth out of the row D X, the fifth out of the row E X, and finally, the sixth out of the row F X.

This being done, you brush together each row of numbers separately, and place the six numbers which form the row A X in such a manner that they will lie in a circle around the central point X, and so that the number 15 will keep its former place ; but in place of number 1 of the next row, B X, you put the number 16 ; in place of the number 14 of the third row, you put the number 28 ; in place of the number 7 of the fourth row, you put the number 34 ; in the place of the number 12 in the fifth row, the number 35 ; and finally, in the place of the number 9 in the sixth row, you put the number 36, so that the six numbers of the first row, A X, will lie one in each of the six rows, and form the number next to X in each row.

Proceed in this way with the six numbers, 1, 13, 11, 31, 33, 32, which form the row B X, so that these shall be distributed in the six rows in a circle, and thus form the second number to X in each row. Proceed in the same manner with the third, fourth, fifth, and sixth rows, and you have the numbers arranged as follows :

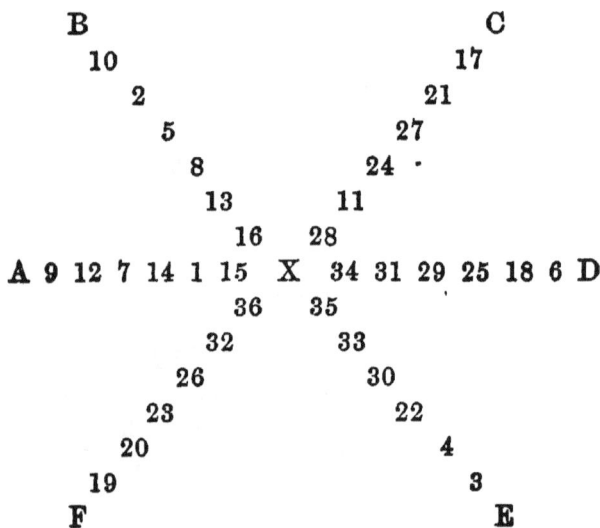

FIG. 50.

When the numbers are arranged in this manner, you ask each of the six persons in which row the number which he had chosen was now to be found, when the number chosen by the person A, in the row A X, will be found to be the first number in the row now pointed out by him, and next to the letter X.

The number chosen by B, from the former row B X, will be the second number from X, in the row which the person points out. In this manner you can easily discover the numbers chosen by the third, fourth, fifth, and sixth persons.

When, for example, the person A declares that the number he had chosen from the row A X, is now in the row E X, he must have chosen the number 35. This mechanical calculation never fails to prove correct, and is therefore a very entertaining amusement.

The Row of Figures.

In what manner can a person reckon up how much the numbers 1, 2, 3, 4, 5, up to 50 amount to, when added together, without adding them up either in your head or upon paper?

Ans.—The first and last of these numbers, 1 and 50, make 51, the second and last but one, 2 and 49, also make 51, and so on through the whole row of figures. Altogether, therefore, there are 25 times 51, which makes 1275.

The Board and Rings.

Procure two small boards about four inches in length, and one inch wide, made of some hard polished wood, furnished at each end with small brass rings, as represented in Fig. 51. Now have a piece of string (not liable to twist) with the ends tied together, and commence operations by passing one end of the double string through the ring F from above downwards; then pass the lower

FIG. 51.

loop over the entire board, and draw it tight by pulling upon the opposite end of the string. Now you have formed the first hitch,

FIG. 52.

as represented in Fig. 52. The puzzle is to form a similar hitch on the farthermost ring of the second board (after passing the double string through the ring E from above downwards, and through the ring D from below upwards, then through the ring C from above downwards). You must proceed in this wise. Pass the loop H over the ring C, and board B, through the ring D, and over the board A; then draw

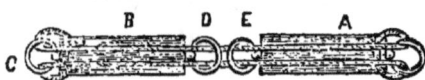

FIG. 53.

the loop, so formed, tight by pulling the boards A and B in opposite directions. You will find you have formed a curiously interlaced mass, as represented by Fig. 53, which but few will be able to disengage.

In order to disentangle it, you must take the loop C, and pass it along the board B, putting it through the ring D. Pass the board through the loop C, and draw your boards in opposite directions again, and you will find you have disentangled one end, and the board B is at liberty. Now the board A can easily be loosened, by simply drawing the loop over the board A, and pulling the double string out. Observe! you will find it as difficult a matter to disentangle the string as it is to put it on in the first place.

Key, Heart, and Arrow.

Cut out of pasteboard an arrow, as seen in Fig. 54, a key, as in Fig. 55, a heart as in Fig. 56. The heart must be cut through in three or four different places as in the plate. These three objects can be put together in such a manner (Fig. 57) that it will be very difficult to separate them, unless a person is acquainted with the method.

You press out the lowermost cut in the heart, so that it forms a loop, which you draw through the ring of the key, so that you can

FIG. 54.   FIG. 55.   FIG. 56.

pass one end of the arrow through it, without breaking the pasteboard.   Then fold the arrow together in the middle, so that one
point shall fit accurately upon the other, bring the loop back into
its former position, drawing it out of the ring of the key, which
then glides down the arrow, and hangs, held fast by its barb, when
the three objects will be joined together as seen in Fig. 57.

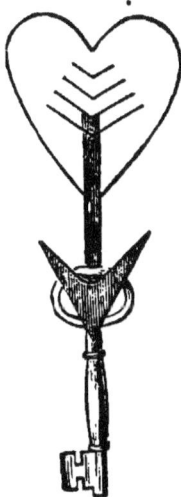

FIG. 57.

The ring of the key should be made quite small, so as to allow
the barb of the arrow to pass through it with some difficulty, and
as no one supposes that it can be taken out in any other manner,
the trick seems the more difficult, as it is forbidden to bend the
pasteboard.

5*

The Perplexed Carpenter.

There is a hole in the barn floor just two feet in width and twelve in length. How can it be entirely covered with a board three feet wide and eight feet long, by *cutting the board only once in two?*

The board was cut after the manner of the annexed diagram:

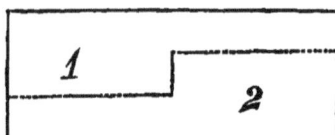

FIG. 58.

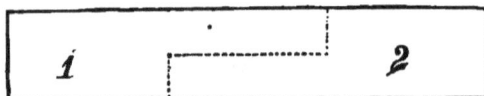

FIG. 59.

Scraps for the Curious.

If a tallow-candle be placed in a gun and shot at a door, it will go through without sustaining any injury; and if a musket-ball be fired into water, it will not only rebound, but be flattened, as if fired against a solid substance.

A musket-ball may be fired through a pane of glass, making the hole the size of the ball, without cracking the glass; if the glass be suspended by a thread it will make no difference, and the thread will not even vibrate.

Cork, if sunk two hundred feet in the ocean, will not rise, on account of the pressure of the water.

In the Arctic regions, when the thermometer is below zero, persons can converse more than a mile distant. Dr. Jamieson asserts that he heard every word of a sermon at the distance of two miles.

To Find six times Thirteen in Twelve

Place your figures thus——

1, 2, 3, 4, 5, 6, 7, 8, 9, 10, 11, 12,

and, taking always the first and the last figure together, you say,

1 and 12 make	13
2 " 11 "	13
3 " 10 "	13
4 " 9 "	13	6 times.
5 " 8 "	13
6 " 7 "	13

A very pretty, and hitherto unknown, Game at Cards, called TONTINE, with which a large Party may be Amused.

(Observe, that the game may be learned in a moment.) This game is played with fifty-two cards. After every person has taken a certain number of counters—say twenty—each one puts three into the pool, and the play may be begun. Some one cuts, and deals one card, face up, to each person; this is the foundation of the game. He to whom a king comes takes three counters; a queen, two; a knave, one. The ten neither takes nor gives, the ace gives one to the next neighbor of the person who holds it; the deuce gives two to the second player above him; the three gives three to the *third* above. For the rest of the cards, the holders pay one or two counters, according as they are even or odd; the four, two; the five, one; the six, two; the seven, one; the eight, two; the nine, one. It will be seen that twenty-four counters are drawn by the players; twenty-four are in circulation, and thirty-six are in the pool. Thus, each time that a round is played, twelve counters leave the hands of the players. When anyone has no more counters, he returns his cards, and is said to be "*dead.*" But he often comes back to life very speedily, since if an ace happens to come to his next neighbor below, that neighbor has to give him a counter: he who is two places below him, will give him two, if a deuce comes to him; and his third neighbor below will have to pay him three, should a card with that number of spots be dealt to him.   This rule causes many fluctuations of fortune.   Finally, the pool belongs to him who has most counters left: but many changes take place before this catastrophe happens; and it is often the player whose circumstances have been most desperate, and who, perhaps, has been two or three times *dead*, who wins the game. The excitement and constant change make this a very amusing game.

To make a Straw Cross Turn, by Pouring on it Two or Three Drops of Water.

Take a blade of straw, from which you will cut a finger length, ard turn the end secretly, before announcing this trick.   When it is turned, with another bit of straw make it into a cross, which you must stick in a crack of the table.   When you pour water on the top of the straw, it penetrates into the bend you have made, which turns; and the cross has the appearance of turning, although in fact it is fixed.

Permutation Table.

Take ten blank cards, on each of which you have written one of the figures, 1, 2, 3, 4, 5, 6, 7, 8, 9, 0.

Take these ten cards in the left hand, as you do when shuffling a pack.   Slip off, without altering their order, the two first cards 1 and 2.   Put above them the following two, 3 and 4 ; and under these four the three following, 5, 6, 7.   Then, at the top of the pack, 8 and 9; with the 0 card at the bottom.   You can shuffle them in the same manner several times.   At each new shuffle you will have a different order, notwithstanding which, after a certain number, they will get into the same order that they held before they were shuffled, as may be seen in the following table, in which, after the seventh shuffle, they return to their first arrangement :—

1st,	1	2	3	4	5	6	7	8	9	0
1st shuffle,	8	9	3	4	1	2	5	6	7	0
2d,	6	7	3	4	8	9	1	2	5	0
3d,	2	5	3	4	6	7	8	9	1	0
4th,	9	1	3	4	2	5	6	7	8	0
5th,	7	8	3	4	9	1	2	5	6	0
6th,	5	6	3	4	7	8	9	1	2	0
7th,	1	2	3	4	5	6	7	8	9	0.

An Extremely Amusing Trick.

Place two persons on their knees, opposite to each other; each is to kneel on one knee, with the other leg in the air. Give to one of them a lighted candle, requesting him to light that of the other person. This is exceedingly difficult to do, both being poised in equilibrium on one knee, and liable to tumble down at the slightest disarrangement of position.

Peculiar Properties of the Numbers 37 and 73.

The number 37 is one which being multiplied by each of the figures of arithmetical progression, 3, 6, 9, 12, 15, 18, 21, 24, 27, all the products which result from it are composed of three repetitions of the same figure; and the sum of these figures is equal to that by which you multiplied the 37.

37	37	37	37	37	37	37	37	37
3	6	9	12	15	18	21	24	27
111	222	333	444	555	666	777	888	999

The number 73, multiplied by each of the numbers of arithmetical progression, 3, 6, 9, 12, 15, 18, 21, 24, and 27, the six products which result from this multiplication are terminated by one of the nine different figures, 1, 2, 3, 4, 5, 6, 7, 8, 9. These figures will be found in the reverse order to that of the progression.

Two Dice being thrown on the Table, to find out the Spots on them without seeing them.

Tell the person who threw the dice to add *five* to double the number of spots on one of them; and then to multiply the whole by the same number, 5. Make him add to this product the number of spots on the other die; and ask him to tell you the amount of the whole. Subtract *twenty-five*, which is the square of the number five, and there will remain two numbers or figures, of which the one that represents the tens indicates the number of the first die, and that of the units will be the amount of the second.

EXAMPLE.

We will suppose the throw was 2, 6.

The double of the first is	4
Add	5
	—
Total	9
Multiply by 5	5
	—
Product	45
Add the spots on the second . . .	6
	—
	51
Subtract	25
	—
	26

We know that these two figures 2 and 6 were those of the throw.

To Show some Worms in a Bottle after having put into it Earth and Water.

Take a wide-mouthed bottle, in which you put earth and water, and have a hollow cork in it. Fill the hollow lightly with small scrapings of horn, and bits of the catgut used for violin strings. Stop up the hollow with a bit of sugar. Set the bottle in a pan of water on the fire; and when it heats the water in the bottle, the sugar will melt, and drop in, and, with it, the filings and bits of catgut that were placed in the cork. The heat will make them roll about, and give them all the appearance of living worms.

Piquet on Horseback.

Two gentlemen, travelling on horseback, and tired of their journey, may amuse themselves and beguile the time by counting up a hundred, as at piquet without cards, agreeing that he who first reaches 100 shall be considered to have won; and that, in counting alternately, each is at liberty to add whatever he pleases, provided it does not exceed eleven.

You must first understand the peculiar properties of the number 11, which, multiplied by the terms of arithmetical progression, 1, 2, 3, 4, 5, 6, 7, 8, and 9, always gives, as a product, two similar figures.

EXAMPLE.

11	11	11	11	11	11	11	11	11
1	2	3	4	5	6	7	8	9
11	22	33	44	55	66	77	88	99

In order, then, that the one who names the first number should be able to arrive first at 100, and that his opponent should not be able to do so, he must bear in mind all these products, and count in such a manner that he should find himself always one unit above these products, having taken care to name *one* first. His adversary being debarred from taking a higher number than *ten*, he cannot get to twelve which the first speaker must make up, and afterwards the numbers, 23, 34, 45, 56, 67, 78, 89. When he has reached this last, whatever number the opponent may choose, cannot prevent him from reckoning 100 first, and consequently winning the game.

To ensure winning, it is advisable to master and remember the numbers to be made in the retrograde order also; 89, 78, 67, 56, 45, 34, 23, 12, 1.

Mode of Printing a Card on a White Handkerchief.

Before performing this trick, you borrow several handkerchiefs, under different pretexts, and keep them at least five minutes on your table; put your own among them, unobserved, in order to be able, afterwards, to take one away, and still leave the same number; as you will not be able to make use of your own. Then give a pack of cards up to be shuffled. Under pretence that you do not wish to be present while the shuffling is going on, you go into another apartment. You have a copper stencil-plate, representing the eight of diamonds or hearts, or a club or spade, without any border or ornament. Any card, indeed, will do, except the ace or a picture card. With one of the brushes which are bought at the stencil-plate makers, manufactured for the purpose you print the card lightly on the middle of the handkerchief. Rea cards are printed with vermilion, moistened with isinglass; the black is produced by charcoal, mixed into a liquid in the same way. When the pack has been shuffled, you return all the handkerchiefs, with the exception of the printed one, which you place on the table, spreading out your pack on it. When you recognise your card, put it on the top of the pack, making the pass afterwards, so that it will be in the middle. You take it out, and burn it, then load a pistol with powder only, and having assured yourself that the card is completely burned, you put the ashes into the pistol, fold the handkerchief so that the impression is on the inside, fire off the pistol, and at the moment of the explosion, open the handkerchief, when the card will appear on it.

THE END

Popular Books sent Free of Postage at the prices annexed.

The Sociable; *or, One Thousand and One Home Amusements.* Containing Acting Proverbs, Dramatic Charades, Acting Charades, Tableaux Vivants, Parlor Games, and Parlor Magic, and a choice collection of Puzzles, &c., illustrated with nearly 300 Engravings and Diagrams, the whole being a fund. of never-ending entertainment. By the Author of the "Magician's Own Book." Nearly 400 pages, 12mo., cloth, gilt side stamp........................Price $1.25.

Inquire Within *for Anything You Want to Know; or, Over 3,700 Facts for the People.* Illustrated, 436 large pages...Price $1.25.

"Inquire Within" is one of the most valuable and extraordinary volumes ever presented to the American public, and embodies nearly 4,000 facts, in most of which any person living will find instruction, aid, and entertainment. It contains so many valuable and useful recipes, that an enumeration of them requires *seventy-two columns of fine type for the Index.*

The Corner Cupboard; *or, Facts for Everybody.* By the Author of "Inquire Within," "The Reason Why," &c. Large 12mo., 400 pages, cloth, gilt side and back. Illustrated with over 1000 Engravings.
Price $1.25.

The Reason Why: *General Science.* A careful collection of some thousands of reasons for things, which, though generally known, are imperfectly understood. By the Author of "Inquire Within." A handsome 12mo. volume of 356 pages, cloth, gilt, and embellished with a large number of wood-cuts....................Price $1.25.

The Biblical Reason Why: A Hand-Book for Biblical Students, and a Guide to Family Scripture Readings. By the Author of "Inquire Within, &c. Beautifully illustrated, large 12mo. cloth, gilt side and back..Price $1.25.

The Reason Why: *Natural History.* By the Author of "Inquire Within," "The Biblical Reason Why," &c. 12mo. cloth, gilt side and back. Giving Reasons for hundreds of interesting facts in Natural History..Price $1.25.

10,000 Wonderful Things. Comprising the Marvellous and Rare, Odd, Curious, Quaint, Eccentric, and Extraordinary, in all Ages and Nations, in Art, Nature, and Science. including many Wonders of the world, enriched with Hundreds of Authentic Illustrations. 12mo. cloth, gilt side and back............................Price $1.25.

That's It; *or, Plain Teaching* By the Author of "Inquire Within," "The Reason Why," &c. Illustrated with over 1,200 Wood-cuts. 12mo. cloth, gilt side and back......................Price $1.25.

The Lady's Manual of Fancy Work A Complete Instructor in every variety of Ornamental Needle-Work; including Shading and Coloring, Printer's Marks, Explanatory Terms, &c., &c. The Whole being a Complete Lexicon of Fancy Work. By Mrs. PULLAN, Director of the Work-table of Frank Leslie's Magazine, &c., &c. Illustrated with over 300 Engravings, by the best Artists, with eight large pattern plates, elegantly printed in colors on tinted paper. Large 8vo., beautifully bound in fine cloth, with gilt side and back stamp.
Price $1.25.

Popular Books sent Free of Postage at the prices annexed.

Live and Learn : A Guide for all those who wish to speak and write correctly ; particularly intended as a Book of Reference for the solution of difficulties connected with Grammar, Composition, Punctuation, &c., &c., containing examples of one thousand mistakes of daily occurrence, in speaking, writing, and pronunciation. 216 pages, cloth, 12mo...Price 63 cts.

The Harp of a Thousand Strings ; or, *Laughter for a Lifetime.* A large book of nearly 400 pages. By the Author of Mrs. Partington's Carpet-Bag of Fun." Bound in a handsome gilt cover. Containing more than a million laughs, and crowded full of Funny Stories, besides being illustrated with over Two Hundred Comical Engravings, by Darley, McLennan, Bellew, &c......................Price $1.25.

The Book of 1.000 Comical Stories ; or. *Endless Repast of Fun.* Appropriately illustrated with 300 Comic Engravings. By the Author of " Mrs. Partington's Carpet Bag of Fun." Large 12mo. cloth.
Price $1.00.

The Perfect Gentleman ; or, *Etiquette and Eloquence.* A Book of Information and Instruction for those who desire to become brilliant and conspicuous in General Society ; or at Parties, Dinners, or Popular Gatherings. Containing Model Speeches for all Occasions, with Directions how to deliver them ; 500 Toasts and Sentiments for everybody, and their proper mode of introduction ; How to use Wine at Table ; with Rules for judging the quality of Wine, and Rules for Carving ; Etiquette, or proper Behavior in Company, with an American Code of Politeness for every Occasion ; Etiquette at Washington, Remarkable Wit and Conversation at Table, &c., &c. To which is added, The Duties of a Chairman of a Public Meeting, with Rules for the Orderly Conduct thereof ; together with Valuable Hints and Examples for Drawing up Preambles and Resolutions, and a great deal of instructive and amusing matter never before published. 12mo. cloth, nearly 400 pages................................Price $1.25.

Songs of Ireland : Embracing Songs of the Affections, Convivial and Comic Songs, Patriotic and Military Songs ; Historical and Political Songs ; Moral, Sentimental, Satirical, and Miscellaneous Songs. Edited and Annotated by Samuel Lover, Author of "Handy Andy," "Rory O'More," "Legends and Stories of Ireland," &c. Embellished with numerous fine Illustrations, engraved by the celebrated Dalziel. 12mo. cloth, gilt side and back......................Price $1.25.

Narratives and Adventures of Travelers in Africa. By Charles Williams, Esq. 12mo. cloth, gilt back. Profusely illustrated with Engravings..Price $1.00.

The Lady's Own Pattern Book ; or, *Treasures in Needlework.* Comprising instructions in Knitting, Netting, Crochet, Point Lace. Tatting, Braiding, Embroidery, &c. Illustrated with over Five Hundred Useful and Ornamental Designs, Patterns, &c. By Mrs. Pullan and Mrs. Warren. Large 12mo. gilt side and back. This work, which is superbly gotten up, so as to fit it for holiday *souvenirs*, contains over Five Hundred Engravings, Pattern Plates, &c., and besides, embraces minute instructions for the execution of every known species of needle-work. No family should be without it.........Price $1.25.

Anecdotes of Love. Being a true account of the most remarkable events connected with the History of Love in all Ages and among all Nations. By Lola Montez. Countess of Landsfeldt. Large 12mo, cloth.
Price $1.25.

Send cash orders to **Dick & Fitzgerald, 18 Ann St., N. Y.**

Popular Books sent Free of Postage at the prices annexed.

The Book of 500 Curious Puzzles. Containing a large collection of Entertaining Paradoxes, Perplexing Deceptions in Numbers and Amusing Tricks in Geometry. By the author of "The Sociable." Illustrated with a great variety of engravings. 12mo, fancy paper cover --Price 25 cts.

The Book of Fireside Games: A Repertory of Social Amusements. Containing an Explanation of the most Entertaining Games, suited to the Family Circle as a Recreation. By the Author of "The Sociable," "The Secret Out," &c., &c. Illustrated, 12mo, fancy paper cover--Price 25 cts.

The American Home Cook-Book. Containing several hundred excellent Recipes. The whole based on many years' experience of an American Housewife. Illustrated with Engravings. All the Recipes in this Book are written from actual experiments in Cooking. There are no copyings from theoretical cooking recipes. It is a book of 128 pages, and is very cheap.----------------------------Price 25 cts.

Dr. Valentine's Comic Lectures. A budget of Wit and Humor; or, Morsels of Mirth for the Melancholy. A certain cure for the blues, and all other serious complaints. Comprising Comic Lectures on Heads, Faces, Noses, Mouths, Animal Magnetism, etc., with Specimens of Eloquence, Transactions of Learned Societies, Delineations of Eccentric Characters, Comic Songs, etc., etc. By Dr. W. VALENTINE, the favorite delineator of Eccentric Characters. Illustrated with twelve portraits of Dr. Valentine, in his most celebrated characters. 12mo, cloth, gilt.------------------------------- ---------Price 75 cts.
Ornamental paper cover-----------------------------Price 50 cts.

Dr Valentine's Comic Metamorphoses. Being the second series of Dr. Valentine's Lectures, with characters as given by the late Yankee Hill. Embellished with numerous portraits. Ornamental paper cover --------------- ---------------------------Price 50 cts.
Cloth, gilt.--Price 75 cts.

The Book of 1,000 Comical Stories; or, *Endless Repast of Fun.* A rich banquet for every day in the year, with several courses and a dessert. BILL OF FARE: Comprising Tales of Humor, Laughable Anecdotes, Irresistible Drolleries, Jovial Jokes, Comical Conceits, Puns and Pickings, Quibbles and Queries, Bon Mots and Broadgrins, Oddities, Epigrams, &c., &c. Appropriately Illustrated with 300 Comic Engravings. By the author of "Mrs. Partington's Carpet-Bag of Fun." Large 12mo, cloth----------------------------------Price $1.00.

The Courtship and Adventures of Jonathan Homebred; or, *the Scrapes and Escapes of a Live Yankee.* Beautifully Illustrated. 12mo, cloth. The book is printed in handsome style, on good paper, and with amusing engravings--------------------Price $1.00.

Etiquette and the Usages of Society. Containing the most Approved Rules for Correct Conduct in Social and Fashionable Life—with Hints to both Gentlemen and Ladies on Awkward and Vulgar Habits. Also, the Etiquette of Love and Courtship, Marriage Etiquette, &c., &c. By H. P. WILLIS. A book of 64 pages.........Price 10 cts.
Bound in cloth with gilt side, and printed on fine paper, suitable for a present to a lady.-----------------------------------Price 25 cts.

The Chairman and Speaker's Guide ; or, *Rules for the Orderly Conduct of Public Meetings.*----------------------------Price 12 cts.

Popular Books sent Free of Postage at the prices annexed.

Pettengill's Perfect Fortune-Teller and Dream-Book: *or, The Art of Discerning Future Events,* as practiced by Modern Seers and Astrologers—being also a Key to the Hidden Mysteries of the Middle Ages. To which is added Curious and Amusing Charms, Invocations, Signs, &c., &c. By PELETIAH PETTENGILL, Philom. A book of 144 pages, bound in boards, with cloth back ....Price 30 cts.

Courtship Made Easy; *or, The Art of Making Love fully Explained.* Containing full and minute directions for conducting a Courtship with Ladies of every age and position in society, and valuable information for persons who desire to enter the marriage state. Also, Forms of Love Letters to be used on certain occasions. 64 pp. Price 12 cts.

Chesterfield's Art of Letter-writing Simplified. A Guide to Friendly, Affectionate, Polite, and Business Correspondence....Price 12 cts.

Containing a large collection of the most valuable information relative to the Art of Letter-Writing, with clear and complete instructions how to begin and end correspondence, Rules for Punctuation and Spelling, &c., together with numerous examples of Letters and Notes on every subject of Epistolary Intercourse, with several Important Hints on Love Letters.

Knowlson's Farrier, *and Complete Horse Doctor.* We have printed a new and revised edition of this celebrated book, which contains Knowlsons famous Recipe for the cure of Spavin, and other new matter. It is positively the best book of the kind ever written. We sell it cheap because of the immense demand for it. The farmers and horse-keepers like it because it gives them plain common-sense directions how to manage their horses. We sell our new edition (64 pages, 18mo,) cheap --Price 12 cts.

The Art of Conversation : With Remarks on Fashion and Address. By MRS. MABERLY. This is the best book on the subject ever published. It contains nothing that is verbose or difficult to understand, but all the instructions and rules for conversation are given in a plain and common-sense manner, so that any one, however dull, can easily comprehend them. 64 pages octavo, large---------Price 25 cts.

Horse-Taming by a New Method, *as Practiced by J. S. Rarey.* A New and Improved Edition, containing Mr. Rarey's whole Secret of Subduing and Breaking Vicious Horses, together with his Improved Plan of Managing Young Colts, and Breaking them to the Saddle, the Harness, and the Sulkey—with ten engravings illustrating the process. Every person who keeps a horse should buy this book. It costs but a trifle, and you will positively find it an excellent guide in the management of that noble animal. This is a very handsome book of 64 pages --Price 12 cts.

The Game of Whist: Rules, Directions and Maxims to be observed in playing it. Containing also Primary Rules for Beginners, Explanations and Directions for Old Players, and the Laws of the Game. Compiled from Hoyle and Matthews. Also, Loo, Euchre, and Poker, as now generally played—with an explanation of Marked Cards, &c., &c--Price 12 cts.

The Young Bride's Book: An Epitome of the Social and Domestic Duties of Woman, as the Wife and the Mother. By ARTHUR FREEING. This is one of the best and most useful books ever issued in the cheap form. It is printed in clear and beautiful type, and on fine paper--Price 12 cts.

Popular Books sent Free of Postage at the prices annexed.

Courteney's Dictionary of Abbreviations; Literary, Scientific, Commercial, Ecclesiastical, Military, Naval, Legal and Medical. A book of reference—3,000 abbreviations—for the solution of all literary mysteries. By EDWARD S. C. COURTENEY, Esq. This is a very useful book. Everybody should get a copy...........Price 12 cts.

Blunders in Behavior Corrected......................Price 12 cts.
A concise code of deportment for both sexes. "It will polish and refine either sex, and is Chesterfield superseded.—*Home Companion*.

Five Hundred French Phrases. Adapted for those who aspire to speak and write French correctly.............................Price 12 cts.

How to detect Adulteration in our Daily Food and Drink. A complete analysis of the frauds and deceptions practiced upon articles of consumption, by storekeepers and manufacturers; with full directions to detect genuine from spurious, by simple and inexpensive means..Price 12 cts.

The Young Housekeeper's Book; *or, How to have a Good Living upon a Small Income*...................................Price 12 cts.

How to be Healthy: Being a complete Guide to Long Life. By a Retired Physician......................................Price 12 cts.

How to Cut and Contrive Children's Clothes at a Small Cost With numerous explanatory engravings....................Price 12 cts.

How to Talk and Debate; *or, Fluency of Speech Attained without the Sacrifice of Elegance and Sense.*......................Price 12 cts.

How to Manage Children.............................Price 12 cts.

The Great Wizard of the North's Hand-Book of Natural Magic. Being a series of the newest Tricks of Deception, arranged for Amateurs and Lovers of the Art. By Professor J. H. ANDERSON, the Great Wizard of the North..........................Price 25 cts.

Broad Grins of the Laughing Philosopher. Being a Collection of Funny Jokes, Droll Incidents, and Ludicrous Pictures, that will make you laugh out loud! By PICKLE THE YOUNGER, otherwise called "Little Pickle."....................................Price 12 cts.

The Plate of Chowder: *A Dish for Funny Fellows.* Appropriately illustrated with 100 Comic Engravings. By the Author of "Mrs. Partington's Carpet-Bag of Fun." 12mo, paper cover....Price 25 cts.

Deacon Doolittle's Drolleries. A Collection of Funny and Laughable Stories told by the Deacon, in which he had either acted a part or taken much interest in. This book is got up especially for the benefit of thin and spare people—or for that class of mankind whom it would benefit to "Laugh and Grow Fat." It contains some thirty or forty of the best stories ever invented, full of droll and laughable incidents, calculated to drive away the blues, and to make one in good humor with all mankind...... ....Price 12 cts.

The Laughable Adventures of Messrs. Brown, Jones, & Robinson, showing where they went, and how they went; what they did, and how they did it. With nearly two hundred most thrillingly-comic engravings ....Price 25 cts.

Contents of Dick & Fitzgerald's Dime Song Books. 1

THE FLORENCES' IRISH BOY AND YANKEE GIRL SONGSTER.

CONTENTS :

Copies mailed to any address in the United States, free of postage, upon receipt of ten cents.

THE LOVE AND SENTIMENTAL SONGSTER.

CONTENTS :

Copies mailed to any address in the United States, free of postage, upon the receipt of ten cents.

THE CHARLEY O'MALLEY IRISH SONGSTER.

CONTENTS:

Copies mailed to any address in the United States, free of postage, upon receipt of ten cents.

TONY PASTOR'S COMIC SONGSTER.

CONTENTS:

Copies mailed to any address in the United States, free of postage, upon receipt of ten cents.

THE CAMP-FIRE SONG BOOK.

A collection of Jolly, Patriotic, Convivial, and National Songs, embracing all the Popular Camp and Marching Songs, as sung by our Army.

CONTENTS:

All the above Songs go to Popular and well-known tunes, so that they can easily be sung. Copies mailed to any address in the United States, free of postage, upon receipt of ten cents.

THE SHAMROCK; OR, SONGS OF OLD IRELAND.

CONTENTS :

Copies mailed to any address in the United States, free of postage, upon receipt of ten cents.

Contents of Dick & Fitzgerald's Dime Song Books. 5

FRED MAY'S COMIC IRISH SONGSTER.

CONTENTS:

Beer, Boys, Beer.
Biddy Magee.
Cabbage Green.
Comic Medley.   [Him.
Don't Speak of a Man as You find
Dublin Bay.
Encore verses to Biddy Magee.
Fred May's New Medley.
I Likes a Drop of Good Beer,
  (music.)
I'm a Ranting, Roaring Blade.
I was the Boy for Bewitching them.
Judge not a Man.
Katty Mooney.
Larry Morgan.
Larry O'Brien.
Limerick Races.
One Bottle more.
Paddy Miles.
Paddy's Visit to the Theatre.
Poor Old Sailor.
Priest of the Parish.
Quiet Lodgings.

Sal Sly and Billy Snivel.
Simon the Cellarer.
Smuggler King.
St. Keren and King O'Toole.
Teddy O'Neil.
The Black Flag floating gallantly.
The Gay Girls of New York.
The Irish Janius.
The Land of My Birth.
The Learned Man.
The Old Farm Gate.
The Old Maid and her Tom Cat.
The Old Musqueteer.
The Pope He leads a Happy Life.
The Rambling Boy.
The Rambling Boy of Dublin.
The Workhouse Boy.
Toasts and Sentiments.
True-born Irishman.
Very Polite of Her.
Watchman.
What are You Crying for, Nelly.
With a Jolly Full Bottle.

Copies mailed to any address in the United States, free of postage, upon receipt of ten cents.

WOOD'S MINSTREL SONG BOOK.

CONTENTS:

Aunt Dina Roe.
Brudder Bone's Love Scrape.
Charleston Gals.
Colored Fancy Ball.
Colored Orphan Boy.
Cynthia Sue.
De Old Jaw Bone.
De Singing Darkey ob de Ohio.
Dina's Wedding.
Ellen Bayne.
Emma Snow.
Female Slave's Lament.
Fireman's Death, (music.)
Forty-five Jokes and Conundrums.
Gal from the South.
Ginger's Wedding.
Good Old Hut at Home
Guinea Maid.
Hail! All Hail!
I wish I was in Old Virginia.
Jane Munroe.
Jolly Old Crow.
Julius Cæsar Green.
Julius' Bride.
Kate Loraine, (music.)

Katy Darling, (music.)
Listen to the Mocking Bird.
Lubly Colored Dine.
Lubly Dinah.
Nancy Till.
New York by Moonlight.
O'er the Hills, Bessie.
Poor Uncle Tom.
Romping Nell, (music.)
Rosa May.
Rosy Anna.
Sally White.
Susey Brown.
The Age of Humbug.
The Locust Hum.
Uncle Gabriel ; or, Sandy Point.
Wake Up, Mose.
We are gwan to de Shucking.
Where is the Spot that we were
  Born on.
Where is my Pompey Gone!
Would I were a Boy again.
Wood's Delineators.
Young Folks at Home.

Copies mailed to any address in the United States, free of postage, en receipt of ten cents.

THE FRISKY IRISH SONGSTER.

CONTENTS :

An Irishman's Excuse for a Fight;
  or, Thread on the Tail of my
  Coat.
A Tight Irish Heart for the Ladies
Ballinamana Oro.
Barrel of Pork.
Batch of Cakes.
Biddy Maguire of Ballinaclash.
Bryan O'Lynn.
Cruiskeen Lawn.
Dolly Dunn of Donnybrook.
Don't You Think She Did.
Friend, by my Sowl, I'll Whisky
  Drink.
Gaffer Gray.
Going Home with the Milk in the
  Morning.
Handy Andy.
Hoppy Hoolahan's Lament on the
  Death of His Duck.
Horticultural Wife.
Jeff Davis.
Larry McHale.
Murrough O'Monahan.
Murthough Delany's Birth.
Nell Flaugherty's Drake.
Paddy Goshlow.
Paddy's Grave.
Pat and the Priest.

Petticoat Lane.
Robinson Crusoe.
Shcelah O'Neal.
Soldier's Dream.
Sprig of Shillelah.
Summer Hill Courtship.
The Anchor's Weighed.
The Bells of Shandon.
The Freemason.
The Great, Big, Ugly Irishman.
The Guager's Slip.
The Humors of Passage.
The Hungry Army.
The Jolly Beggar.
The Land of Shillelah.
The Man in the Moon.
The Miller's Song.
The Muleteer.
The New York Volunteer.
The Pirate Crew.
The Stars and Stripes.
The Wedding of Ballyporeen.
The Widow that Keeps the Cock
  Inn.
The Wild Irishman.
There's Room for All.
Useful Knowledge.
What an Illigant Life a Friar Leads
Young Volunteer.

Copies mailed to any address in the United States, free of postage,
upon receipt of ten cents.

GUS SHAW'S COMIC SONG BOOK.

CONTENTS :

Alonzo, the Brave.
Shells of Oysters.
The Bill-Poster.
Mr. and Mrs. Snibbs.
Nora Daley.
St. Patrick's Birth-Day.
The Female Smuggler.
The Lively Flea.
Sights for a Father.
Nepoletaine.
My Mother was a True Born
  Irishman.
Paper Song.
Mr. and Mrs. Bone.
Robin Ruff and Gaffer Green.
Root, Hog, or Die.

Rat Catcher's Daughter.
Larboard Watch.
Larry O'Brien.
The Irishman's Shanty.
New York in Slices.
Hamlet—A Tragedy.
Nonsense.
Bumper of Lager.
Brogue and Blarney.
My Mary's Nose.
Fair of Clogheen.
Billy Nutts, the Poet.
In the Days when I was Hard Up.
The Irish Jaunting Car.
Wooden Leg Sailor.
The Sicilian Maid.

Copies mailed to any address in the United States, free of postage,
upon receipt of ten cents.

WOOD'S NEW PLANTATION MELODIES.

CONTENTS :

Copies mailed to any address in the United States, free of postage, on receipt of ten cents.

---◆---

HARRISON'S COMIC SONGSTER.

CONTENTS :

Copies mailed to any address in the United States, free of postage, upon receipt of ten cents.

TONY PASTOR'S UNION SONG BOOK. .

CONTENTS :

"Any other Man"
As I went Walking on ; or, a Trip through Broadway
A Warmer
Couldn't see the Point
"Freemen, Rally"
How are you, "Hold Hingland!"
Hunkey Boy is Yankee Doodle
March for the Union
McFay on McClellan
Old England's Position
Old Johnny Bull has raised his Ire
Onward March to Victory
Our Four-and-Thirty Stars
Sumter, the Shrine of the Nation
That Southern Wagon
That's what's the Matter, No. 1
    "   "   "   " No. 2
The Confederate Carnival
The Fall of Lander
The Fishball Musketeer
The Irish Volunteer
The March of the Union

The Monitor and Merrimac
The New Ballad of Lord Lovell
The New England Boys
The New Whack Row de Dow
The Peaceful Battle of Manassas
The Poor Old Worn-out Traitor
The Standard of Freedom
The Union Big Thing on Ice
The Union Bridge
The Union Train
The Union Volunteers
The Yankee's Escape from Secesh
Things I Do Like to See
Tony's Great Union Speech
To the Girl I left Behind
Uncle Sam in for the Union, and out against Disunion
Uncle Sam "Under Weigh"
Union Speech, No. 2
We are Marching to the War
Whack Row de Dow, (new version)
When this Old Hat was New
Ye Sons of Columbia

Copies mailed to any address in the United States, free of postage upon receipt of ten cents.

BOB HART'S PLANTATION SONGSTER.

CONTENTS :

African Statues
Adventures on Staten Island
Adolphus Snow
Around the Horn
Abraham Brown
Bride of Rinaldo
Bryan O'Lynn, (new version)
Come Jeff, Come
Cruelty to Johnny
Con Donahue
Charcoal Man
Can't Stand the Press, (new version)
Deceitful Maiden   [Speech"
Dat's What's the Matter. "Stump
Disappointed Lovyer
Down the River
Dutchman's Shanty
Encore Verses, "Sally, come Up"
Freezing Bed-Fellow
Farmer's Daughter
Gray Mare
Get Up and Git
Gay Cavalier
Goose Hangs High, (new version)
Gay City Conductor
Ham Fat Man
Happy Contraband
Home in Kentuck

Hart's "Original Burlesque Speech"
Jeff Davis's Dream
Joe Bowers
Little Pigs
Mount Vernon
Mickey's Gone Away
Negro Lecture
    "   Stump Speech
Private Maguire
Patriotic Song
Peter Gray
Peanut Girl
Putting on Airs
Rip, Tare, my Johnny
Radish Girl
Row the Boat
Soap-Fat Man
Sally come Up
The Three Black Crows
The Gabble Family
The Dog is Dead
The Groceryman
Uncle Snow
Union Song
Young Bob Ridley
Young Volunteer
Van Amburgh's Menagerie.

Copies mailed to any address in the United States, free of postage, upon receipt of ten cents.

BOOK of RIDDLES
500 HOME AND AMUSEMENTS

NEW YORK:

DICK & FITZGERALD, PUBLISHERS.

POPULAR BOOKS

SENT FREE OF POSTAGE AT THE PRICES ANNEXED.

The Sociable; or, *One Thousand and One Home Amusements*. Containing Acting Proverbs, Dramatic Charades, Acting Charades, Tableaux Vivants, Parlor Games and Parlor Magic, and a choice collection of Puzzles, &c., illustrated with nearly 300 Engravings and Diagrams, the whole being a fund of never-ending entertainment. By the author of the "Magician's Own Book." Nearly 400 pages. 12mo., cloth, gilt side stamp...................................**Price $1 00.**

Inquire Within *for Anything You Want to Know; or, Over 3,700 Facts for the People.* Illustrated, 436 large pages......... .... **Price $1 00.**

"Inquire Within" is one of the most valuable and extraordinary volumes ever presented to the American public, and embodies nearly 4.000 facts, in most of which any person living will find instruction, aid, and entertainment. It contains so many valuable and useful recipes, that an enumeration of them requires *seventy-two columns of fine type for the Index.*

The Corner Cupboard; or, *Facts for Everybody*. By the Author of "Inquire Within," "The Reason Why," &c. Large 12mo., 400 pages, cloth, gilt side and back. Illustrated with over 1000 Engravings.........**Price $1 00.**

The Reason Why: *General Science.* A careful collection of some thousands of reasons for things, which, though generally known, are imperfectly understood. By the Author of "Inquire Within." A handsome 12mo volume of 356 pages, cloth, gilt, and embellished with a large number of wood cuts.
Price $1 00.

The Biblical Reason Why: A Hand-Book for Biblical Students, and a Guide to Family Scripture Readings. By the Author of "Inquire Within," &c. Beautifully illustrated, large 12mo., cloth, gilt side and back,.....**Price $1 00.**

The Reason Why: *Natural History.* By the Author of "Inquire Within," "The Biblical Reason Why," &c. 12mo, cloth, gilt side and back. Giving Reasons for hundreds of interesting facts in Natural History.
Price $1 00.

10,000 Wonderful Things. Comprising the Marvellous and Rare, Odd, Curious, Quaint, Eccentric and Extraordinary, in all Ages and Nations, in Art, Nature and Science, including many Wonders of the world, enriched with Hundreds of Authentic Illustrations. 12mo, cloth, gilt side and back.
Price $1 00.

That's It; or, *Plain Teaching*. By the Author of "Inquire Within," "The Reason Why," &c. Illustrated with over 1,200 Wood-cuts. 12mo., cloth, gilt side and back,...**Price $1 00.**

The Lady's Manual of Fancy Work: A complete Instructor in every variety of Ornamental Needle Work; including Shading and Coloring, Printers' Marks, Explanatory Terms, &c., &c. The whole being a complete Lexicon of Fancy Work. By Mrs. PULLAN, Director of the Work-table of Frank Leslie's Magazine, &c., &c. Illustrated with over 300 Engravings, by the best artists, with eight large pattern plates, elegantly printed in colors, on tinted paper. Large 8vo, beautifully bound in fine cloth, with gilt side and back stamp, **Price $1 25.**

Live and Learn: A Guide for all who wish to Speak and Write correctly; particularly intended as a Book of Reference for the solution of difficulties connected with Grammar, Composition, Punctuation, &c, &c., containing examples of one thousand mistakes of daily occurrence, in speaking, writing, and pronunciation. 216 pages, cloth, 12mo.................................**Price 50 cts.**

The Harp of a Thousand Strings; or, *Laughter for a Lifetime* A large book of nearly 400 pages. By the author of Mrs. Partington's Carpet Bag of Fun. Bound in a handsome gilt cover. Containing more than a million laughs, and crowded full of Funny Stories, besides being illustrated with over Two Hundred Comical Engravings, by Darley McLennan, Bellew, &c.,.....**Price $1 25.**

The Book of 1,000 Comical Stories; or, *Endless Repast of Fun*. Appropriately illustrated with 300 Comic Engravings. By the Author of "Mrs. Partington's Carpet Bag of Fun. Large 12mo., cloth,........**Price $1 00.**

Send Cash Orders to   **DICK & FITZGERALD, 18 Ann St., N. Y.**

GOOD BOOKS

SENT FREE OF POSTAGE AT THE PRICES MARKED.

Send Cash Orders to

DICK & FITZGERALD, Publishers,
No. 18 ANN STREET, NEW YORK.

POPULAR BOOKS

The Secret Out; *or, One Thousand Tricks with Cards and other Recreations.* Illustrated with over Three Hundred Engravings. A book which explains all the Tricks and Deceptions with Playing Cards ever known or invented, and gives, besides, a great many new and interesting ones—the whole being described so accurately and carefully, with engravings to illustrate them, that anybody can easily learn how to practice these Tricks. This Work also contains 240 of the best tricks in Legerdemain, in addition to the card tricks. 12mo., 400 pages, bound in cloth, with gilt side and back................................**Price $1 00.**

The Art of Dancing. Containing the Figures, Music, and necessary Instruction for all Modern Approved Dances. Also, Hints on Etiquette, and the Ethics of Politeness. By Edward Ferrero, Professor of Dancing, &c., &c. A large bound book, full of Engravings and Music to illustrate it,........**Price $1 00.**

The Dictionary of Love. Containing a Definition of all the terms used in Courtship, with rare quotations from Poets of all Nations, together with specimens of curious model Love-Letters, and many other interesting matters appertaining to Love, never before published. 12mo., cloth, gilt side and back.
Price $1 00.

The Magician's Own Book : Being a Hand-Book of Parlor Magic, and containing several hundred amusing Magical, Magnetical, Electrical, and Chemical Experiments, Astonishing Transmutations, Wonderful Sleight-of-hand and Card Tricks, Curious and Perplexing Puzzles, Quaint Questions in Numbers &c., together with all the most noted Tricks of Modern Performers. Illustrated with over 500 Wood Engravings. 12mo., cloth, gilt side and back stamp, 400 pages,
Price $1 00.

Anecdotes of Love. Being a true account of the most remarkable events connected with the History of Love in all Ages and among all Nations. By LOLA MONTEZ, Countess of Landsfeldt. Large 12mo., cloth,.....**Price $1 00.**

The Book of 1,000 Tales and Amusing Adventures. Containing over 300 Engravings, and 450 pages. This is a magnificent book, and is crammed full of narratives and adventures......................**Price $1 00.**

The Bordeaux Wine and Liquor Dealer's Guide: *or, How to Manufacture and Adulterate Liquors.* By a practical Liquor Manufacturer. 12mo., cloth,..**Price $1 50.**
In this work. *not one* article in the smallest degree approximating to a poison, is recommended, and yet the book teaches how Cognac Brandy, Scotch and Irish Whiskey, Foreign and Domestic Rum, all kinds of Wines, Cordials, &c., from the choicest to the commonest, can be imitated to that perfection, that the best judges cannot detect the method of manufacture, even by *chemical tests of the severest character.*

Ladies' Guide to Crochet. By Mrs. Ann S. Stephens. Copiously illustrated with original and very choice designs in Crochet, etc., printed in colors, separate from the letter press, on tinted paper. Also with numerous wood-cuts, printed with the letter-press, explanatory of terms, etc. Oblong, pp. 117, beautifully bound in extra cloth, gilt. This is by far the best work on the subject of Crochet, yet published..................................**Price 75 cts.**

Arts of Beauty ; *or, Secrets of a Lady's Toilet.* With Hints to Gentlemen on the Art of Fascinating. By Madame LOLA MONTEZ, Countess of Landsfeldt. Cloth, gilt side. This book contains an account, in detail, of all the arts employed by the fashionable ladies of all the chief cities of Europe, for the purpose of developing and preserving their charms................ ....**Price 50 cts.**

Courtship Made Easy ; *or, The Art of Making Love fully Explained.* Containing full and minute Directions for conducting a Courtship with Ladies of every age and position in Society, and valuable information for persons who desire to enter the marriage state. Also, Forms of Love Letters to be used on certain occasions. A book of 64 pages...........................**Price 13 cts.**

Send cash orders to   **DICK & FITZGERALD, 18 Ann St., N. Y.**

www.ingramcontent.com/pod-product-compliance
Lightning Source LLC
Chambersburg PA
CBHW031439280326
41927CB00038B/1130